Frank Henderson's ~~~~
Recollections of a Dublin Volunteer

IRISH NARRATIVES

IRISH NARRATIVES
Series edited by David Fitzpatrick

Personal narratives of past lives are essential for understanding any field of history. They provide unrivalled insight into the day-to-day consequences of political, social, economic or cultural relationships. Memoirs, diaries and personal letters, whether by public figures or obscure witnesses of historical events, will often captivate the general reader as well as engrossing the specialist. Yet the vast majority of such narratives are preserved only among the manuscripts or rarities in libraries and archives scattered over the globe. The aim of this series of brief yet scholarly editions is to make available a wide range of narratives concerning Ireland and the Irish over the last four centuries. All documents, or sets of documents, are edited and introduced by specialist scholars, who guide the reader through the world in which the text was created. The chosen texts are faithfully transcribed, the biographical and local background explored, and the documents set in historical context. This series will prove invaluable for university and school teachers, providing superb material for essays and textual analysis in class. Above all, it offers a novel opportunity for readers interested in Irish history to discover fresh and exciting sources of personal testimony.

Other titles in the series:

Andrew Bryson's Ordeal: An Epilogue to the 1798 Rebellion, edited by Michael Durey
Henry Stratford Persse's Letters from Galway to America, 1821–1832, edited by James L. Pethica and James C. Roy
Memoirs of Joseph Prost: A Redemptorist Missionary in Ireland, 1851–1854, translated and edited by Emmet Larkin and Herman Freudenberger

Forthcoming titles:

A Patriot Priest: A Life of Reverend James Coigly, edited by Dáire Keogh

'My Darling Danny': Letters from Mary O'Connell to her son Daniel, 1830–1832, edited by Erin Bishop

David Fitzpatrick teaches history at Trinity College, Dublin. His books include *Politics and Irish Life, 1913–1921* (1977) and *Oceans of Consolation: Personal Accounts of Irish Migration to Australia* (1995).

Frank Henderson's Easter Rising
Recollections of a Dublin Volunteer

Edited by
Michael Hopkinson

CORK UNIVERSITY PRESS

First published in 1998 by
Cork University Press
Cork
Ireland

© Cork University Press 1998

Reprinted 2008

British Library Cataloguing in Publication Data

A CIP catalogue record for this book is available from the British Library.

ISBN-10: 1 85918 143 0
ISBN-13: 978 1 85918 143 0

Typesetting by Red Barn Publishing, Skeagh, Skibbereen

Contents

Acknowledgements

I am very grateful for the extensive assistance provided by the members of the Henderson family. My thanks also go to the staff of the Archives Department, University College, Dublin, particularly Séamus Helferty, and to the Manuscript Department of the National Library. James McGuire and Diarmuid O'Connor have been invaluable in supplying biographical detail.

Introduction

In recent studies of the Irish Volunteers/IRA during the revolutionary era there has been a stress on the importance of localities and on analysis of the occupational and class background of activists.[1] The move from concentration on the general to the particular has been stimulated by the availability of new sources, including papers supplied by families of IRA veterans, and by changing perspectives resulting from the passage of time.

These memoirs of one of the leading figures of the Dublin Brigade consist firstly of a short, incomplete family narrative which was terminated by Frank Henderson's illness and death in 1959, and of an edited transcription of the first of Henderson's two statements of 1948 to the Bureau of Military History which goes up to Henderson's release from internment in December 1916. (The Bureau of Military History was established in 1947 to collect sworn memoirs of veterans of the revolutionary period. Up to the present the Irish government has not allowed files collected to be made available. Meanwhile historians have gained access to some of these statements by communication with the families involved.) The family memoir was translated from the original Irish by Henderson's son, Father Eanna Henderson. The original script is in the possession of Pádraig Henderson, another of his sons. The statement submitted to the Bureau of Military History was reproduced by the Bureau in the form of a bound typescript. Henderson's second statement to the Bureau is not included for reasons of length and because it was deemed less interesting than the first owing to its concentration on organisational and administrative matters and Henderson's lack of direct involvement in events at the height of the War of Independence. The last two paragraphs of the family memoir have been omitted, as they contain only basic background material relating to Jim Larkin, James Connolly and the Labour movement. Similarly, the first four pages of the Bureau statement have not been included, as they provide merely a brief summary of the historical context. Again, some of the descriptions of training and organisation before the rising in the Bureau statement have been left out. In common with most other Bureau testimonies, Henderson's end during the truce of 1921. It had been Henderson's intention to give an account of his involvement in the Civil War.

Henderson's statement of 1948 gives a straightforward account of his participation in the advanced nationalist cause, followed by a vivid description of the Easter Rising in Fairview (his home area in the north-east of inner-city Dublin), the General Post Office and Henry Street. His narrative is understated and sober, not concerned with self-advertisement or hyperbole.[2]

Valuable comparisons can be made between the two different types of memoir presented in these two documents, and also with the record of Henderson's extended interviews with his fellow IRA veteran Ernie O'Malley, which also date from the late 1940s.[3] The family account is warmer in tone and more revealing than the Bureau statement. Both these documents are generally accurate and reliable, as far as memory allowed. The Bureau account was written for the official record with other IRA veterans in mind; sensitive issues were frequently avoided. Judgements were in line with traditional nationalist assumptions, and little of a critical nature was said about individuals. In the O'Malley interviews, by contrast, Henderson commented that Michael Collins was unpopular in Frongoch internment camp 'and seemed to be looking for power'. Henderson gave a graphic description to O'Malley of Collins in pre-rising days wearing a hard hat, carrying an umbrella and speaking 'bad Irish'. Moreover, Henderson in his discussions with O'Malley often criticised the IRB's influence in a way he avoided in written accounts. Henderson commented on the Treaty split: 'We decided that [the] IRB had done the real damage. It had split the army. They now saw the reason for the Church condemning secret societies.' The following comment on the Dublin 2nd Battalion in the War of Independence contrasts with the cautious character of the Bureau statement: 'In Dublin we didn't call on a lot of men. We were inclined to work in small groups. For when a man was tested and found to be satisfactory he was used again . . . There was a great number of untried men in every Company.'[4] It is invaluable also to relate Henderson's testimony to accounts given by his friends Oscar Traynor[5] and Harry Colley.[6]

A further account by Henderson (together with one by Harry Colley) of their involvement in the Easter Rising is deposited in the National Library of Ireland.[7] This document presents supplementary details and comment on some of the incidents recorded in the Bureau statement; the most significant of these references are indicated in the notes following the statement.

Frank Henderson's memoirs were recommended for publication to coincide with the fiftieth anniversary of the Easter Rising by his old IRA colleague Oscar Traynor, the most likely publisher being the *Irish Press*. At that time the Henderson family decided against publication. In 1989 one of Henderson's sons wrote to the present editor concerning references to his late father in my book *Green against Green: The Irish Civil War*.[8] A wide-ranging correspondence ensued during which the Henderson family sent on a copy of their father's memoirs. When plans for the *Irish Narratives* series were announced, the editor felt that the memoirs were well suited to the project. The Hendersons have provided a considerable amount of detail relating to their father and family and have also supplied a range of photographs.[9] Textual footnotes have been added by the editor to supply, wherever possible, biographical information concerning individuals mentioned.

Much of the Henderson family background is well covered in the family memoir. The Hendersons originally hailed from the Scottish Highlands, where their numbers had been decimated at the massacre of Glencoe. The Protestant ancestry on the male side is unusual, while the lower middle-class background is more typical of many Dublin IRA leaders. Frank Henderson's paternal grandfather had been a successful master saddler and his father a bookbinder in Manchester and Dublin, part of the small-business/skilled-worker culture often associated with Fenian membership. His mother, whose family came from County Armagh, had returned to Ireland from a Fenian background in Manchester. Consultation of the 1911 Census of Ireland in the National Archives confirms that Henderson's mother and her six children lived at 5, Windsor Villas in the Fairview region of Clontarf parish. Henderson's wife, Josephine Ní Bhraonáin (Brennan), originated from County Laois and was related distantly to James Fintan Lalor and Cardinals Cullen and Moran. She met her future husband at Gaelic League meetings, and during the Easter Rising walked across the line of fire from her home in the Arbour Hill area to the General Post Office to bring solace and support. They married in 1918. Henderson's sister Nora was to join the Cumann na mBan and serve in the Four Courts garrison in 1922; she married Joe Tallon, a veteran of the rising. His other sister, Gertie, married Major Leech of the British army and moved to England.

Henderson's younger brother, Leo, was also a leading figure within the Dublin Brigade and was with Frank during the rising and subsequently in Frongoch. He held the rank of captain in the GPO garrison of 1916. The two brothers, however, had an uneasy relationship. Leo was interned in January 1920 and became commandant of the Ballykinlar internees. He became a leading figure among the anti-Treaty Dublin Brigade ranks in 1922, achieving lasting fame as a consequence of his arrest during a raid on a Dublin garage in connection with the Belfast boycott of June 1922 which provided part of the immediate background to the Civil War. Thereafter Leo remained in Mountjoy Prison during the war and was to be in an adjoining cell to Liam Mellows and Rory O'Connor, before their reprisal executions in December 1922.[10] Of the two other brothers, Maurice was also involved in post-1916 Volunteer activity and was interned in 1923 during the Civil War; Robert did not participate in the military struggle.

Henderson's employment career was determined by his association with the nationalist cause. On leaving school at seventeen, he worked in a solicitor's office, losing that job when he refused to take time off to observe Edward VII's visit to Dublin. Because of his political views, he declined to take the civil service entrance examination. Up to the War of Independence he worked as a clerk or accountant in sundry small firms in central Dublin.

Educated at a Christian Brothers' school, Henderson went through a common advanced nationalist apprenticeship — the 'Holy Trinity' of membership of the Gaelic League, the Gaelic Athletic Association and the Irish Volunteers. These organisations required a high degree of commitment among their adherents, often involving considerable personal sacrifice. Membership of the Volunteers meant for Oscar Traynor the end of his professional football career; he had been a goalkeeper with Belfast Celtic.[11] Unlike Traynor, Henderson mastered the Irish language; both Irish and English were spoken in the Henderson home. Henderson was a deeply committed Catholic all his life.

Henderson did, however, show two variations from the norm. First were his socialist sympathies, which owed more to his observation of social injustice in Dublin than to the writings of Marx; in later life he was to name James Connolly as the Irish leader he most admired. In the second place, he did not join the IRB until 1918 and had twice rejected overtures from them. He found it difficult to square secret society membership with his Catholicism. At the start of his family memoir Henderson asserts his love of Dublin and its central role in Irish nationalism. If Todd Andrews had not already used the title *Dublin Made Me* for his autobiography, it would have been highly appropriate for these memoirs.[12]

Henderson joined the Irish Volunteers at the foundation of the organisation in November 1913. Soon after that he attended the first meeting of B Company — later F Company — of the 2nd Battalion, Dublin Brigade, which covered the Fairview and Drumcondra districts. He was present at the Howth gun-running in July 1914, and some of the smuggled arms were hidden under floorboards in the family home in Fairview. At the time of the Volunteer split, which followed the outbreak of the First World War, Henderson estimated that sixty of the company went with Redmond and the National Volunteers and forty remained in the Irish Volunteers. Henderson became captain of F Company in 1915 and Oscar Traynor its first lieutenant.

While Oscar Traynor was to achieve more recognition as Volunteer and politician than Henderson, both personified the intimate connection between IRA service and future social and employment careers. Participation in the rising was to be their major reference-point for the rest of their lives — a guarantee of membership of a nationalist elite, a badge of social and political respectability.

Interned in Stafford jail and Frongoch after the rising, Henderson was released at Christmas 1916. As captain of F Company and then commandant of the 2nd Dublin Battalion covering the north-east of the city, Henderson became, along with Richard Mulcahy, Dick McKee and Oscar Traynor, one of the key figures in the reorganisation of the Dublin Volunteers.[13] They procured arms by various means, organised the funeral of Thomas Ashe, and assisted the emerging Sinn Féin party at by-elections. In early 1918 Henderson was arrested with McKee for drilling in public and imprisoned for two months in Dundalk. He describes in his second Bureau statement McKee's scheme of resisting conscription by occupying blockhouses around Dublin and supported the threats made in 1919–20 to Dublin Metropolitan Police intelligence officers.

When the war escalated in 1920, Henderson's IRA career took a surprising turn. By the time that Traynor replaced McKee as O/C Dublin Brigade, following the latter's death at the hands of British forces in December 1920, Henderson had become attached to the Organisation Department of the IRA's GHQ, with the unfulfilled expectation of becoming its director. The Bureau statement is silent on the reasons for this change in role; but Henderson was to tell Ernie O'Malley that he thought it might have been due to his reluctance to implement a 'shoot-on-sight' policy against policemen. Henderson told O'Malley: 'Some sincere men refused to take part in street ambushes. They had to retire. I never knew of any officer who refused.'[14] As an administrator, Henderson was energetic in working up inactive areas, visiting IRA units in Wicklow, south Kildare, Wexford and Laois. This related well to the importance he always attached to administrative efficiency and kept him in regular contact with the IRA leadership, but meant that he had no first-hand involvement with events in Dublin at the height of the war. Following the decimation of the Dublin Brigade at the botched burning of the Custom House in May 1921, Henderson was recalled to active duty, replacing the wounded Tom Ennis as O/C 2nd Battalion. He helped plan a big offensive against the Auxiliaries in O'Connell Street which was called off because of the truce. Before the signing of the Treaty Henderson became brigade adjutant.

Henderson was an important member of the anti-Treaty IRA. It was he who gave the orders for the Dublin Brigade to assemble immediately before the Provisional Government's attack on the Four Courts, while Traynor was away in Portmarnock. With Traynor he opposed the sacrificial tactics of the Four Courts Executive and strove to implement a plan to hold a ring of buildings on the city's north side during the Dublin fighting while Traynor organised the south side. They soon saw the need to revert to what Henderson called 'the old-time type of fighting', and Henderson set up a full-time Active Service Unit with men paid £1 10s a week. When Traynor was arrested in August 1922, Henderson replaced him as O/C Dublin Brigade and was left to bewail the weaknesses in Republican intelligence which caused the failure of the attempt to isolate the city by blowing up its surrounding bridges on 5 August and the abortive raid soon after on Baldonnel aerodrome.[15] Dublin was not to play an important part in the Civil War after its first few weeks.

When the war turned more bitter after the first executions of Republicans in November 1922, Henderson was extremely reluctant to agree to Liam Lynch's orders to effect an assassination policy directed against TDs who supported the Public Safety Bill. He felt that the government's executions prevented the continuation of Lynch's policy and that there was far more hostility to Republican shootings than to official executions. He therefore told Ernie O'Malley:

> Prominent supporters of the Free State government and Parliament were to have been shot, and it was left to officers in charge of each area who was to have been shot . . . I didn't like that order . . . I could have shot Eamon Duggan and Fionán Lynch, for they went home every night drunk but I left them alone . . . Seán McGarry was

often drunk in Amiens St and the boys wanted to shoot him and the Staters there but I wouldn't let them . . . I think the execution of Rory O'Connor and the others may have stopped a continuation of our shooting. It was very hard to get men to do the shooting and I don't think they'd have done any more shooting.[16]

For the rest of his life it appears that Henderson had on his conscience the orders for the shooting of Pádraic Ó Máille, the Leas-Cheann Comhairle (Deputy Speaker) of the Dáil, and Seán Hales, a pro-Treaty TD and IRA veteran, in early December 1922. It appears that the intention was to kill the former only; in the event, it was Hales who was shot dead, while Ó Máille was wounded. Henderson over a period of sixteen years asked his son to say a mass for Hales. Henderson told O'Malley of a raid on the home of Collins's former intimate, Moya Llewelyn Davies, in January 1923 which unsuccessfully attempted to find a letter from Churchill ordering Collins to attack the Four Courts. Soon after that Henderson was arrested; he was one of the last Republicans to be released in 1924.

It proved difficult to rebuild a civilian career. Henderson's Republican contacts, in professional and social life, enabled him to re-establish himself. He had been unemployed for much of the period of the War of Independence and the Civil War and by 1922 had two children. In 1927 Henderson and Oscar Traynor set up the Fodhla Printing Company, which went bankrupt in 1940. After a short time employed by the Sinn Féin Loan Society, from 1943 to his death in 1959 Henderson was secretary to the Hospital Commission. Henderson and Traynor did not join Fianna Fáil at its foundation in 1926, but were members by 1928. Henderson was a member of the Fianna Fáil National Executive and was co-opted onto Dublin Corporation in 1934. He was a candidate in urban council elections in 1937, unsuccessfully stood for the Senate in 1938,[17] and rejected an approach in 1943 to stand for the Dáil. A reluctant public speaker, he seems to have been ill-at-ease in politics, and far happier in retaining his links with the language movement and becoming a director of the Republican Swimming Club. Henderson was on the visiting committee of Mountjoy Prison in the 1940s and was involved in the military pension scheme. He became a captain and then in 1941 commandant of the 26th Battalion Old IRA during the Second World War. He died in 1959 in his early seventies.

Henderson was keen to avoid post-Civil War bitterness. His family recorded their father's pleasure at a neutrality meeting in 1940 at which old adversaries shared a public platform for the first time since the conflict. Such generosity, however, did not apply to Richard Mulcahy's attitude to Henderson. Mulcahy frequently snubbed him; the family feel that this may have been caused by his holding their father responsible for the killing of Seán Hales and the burning of the TD James McGarry's house in Fairview in December 1922, which resulted in the death of McGarry's young son. Alternatively, it could have been due to tensions from pre-Treaty Dublin Brigade days.

None of the Hendersons' nine children went into politics. All eight boys attended the Christian Brothers' school in Parnell Square. The sole daughter, Nuala, was a pupil at an Irish-speaking school, and became a housewife. Two of the sons became printers, and two became priests, one a horticulturist, one an electrician, and one a school attendance officer. Ruairí, the eldest, became a captain in the Irish army and was one of the first Irish United Nations observers in the Lebanon. On his return to Ireland he was appointed junior aide-de-camp to President de Valera until the latter's retirement, after which he served three further Presidents as senior aide-de-camp. All carried on the family Irish-speaking tradition. Josephine Henderson died in 1971. Oscar Traynor remained a family friend until his death in 1963.

At the start of his family memoir Frank Henderson writes that his civilian career was sacrificed to his nationalist involvement. That was true of many of those on both the pro- and anti-Treaty sides and demonstrates how nationalist conviction dominated lives in the first half of twentieth-century Ireland. For most veterans, association with the events of 1916–21 was the highlight of their lives; it made historically significant men and women who would otherwise be unremarkable. Frank Henderson's memoirs are testimony to the potency of Irish-Ireland principles, and to the close relationship between Catholicism and nationalism. They have importance as social as well as Volunteer history.

Henderson offers no analysis of his reasons for joining the Volunteers. His memoirs, however, do provide an excellent illustration of how family background and social and educational environment conditioned political beliefs. It became customary for the youth of the post-Parnell generation to reject any ambition to progress through the British-controlled system and to stress instead a separate cultural identity. Events between 1912 and 1923 occurred so rapidly that there could be no debate about the precise purpose of the Volunteers or the means which should be used to achieve nationalist demands. Guerrilla warfare tactics emerged as a response to developments and were not part of a prepared policy. Any socialist inclinations were soon overshadowed for most individuals by involvement in the nationalist revolution. Frank Henderson gives a rare demonstrable instance of a questioning attitude to IRA methods. His reservations could not be expressed in his Bureau statements, because this would have been out of step with the prevailing Republican orthodoxy. When he did express such misgivings to Ernie O'Malley, it was in a matter-of-fact manner. Even then, Henderson did not openly state his regret about the Civil War. Through the family memories, however, one gets a touching glimpse of a lasting sadness. Such reflections are a long way removed from the depiction in so many autobiographies and histories of heroic and unblemished freedom-fighters. The reality for individual IRA members was complex and disturbing.

Recollections of Frank Henderson

(1)
'Dad's Personal Reminiscences'
Commenced 8 March 1950

(Translated from the Irish by Rev. Eanna Henderson, O.C.S.O.)

Feast of St John of God and of St Senan
8th day of March, 1950

'Here's to it in God's Name' — for a long time now many people have asked me to put in writing the memoirs of my life in so far as they had reference to the Irish fight for freedom, and those events which inspired me to jeopardise my earthly life, my vocation and the means of livelihood of my mother, my wife and children for the sake of that cause. The last person to ask me to do this was my fourth eldest son, Fr Eanna, O.C.S.O.[1] This was not his first time to ask me but on this particular occasion he did so immediately after his ordination to the priesthood (25th January 1950) and who could refuse a request on such an occasion?

I will try to write down all I have to say in Irish because I have loved it from an early age. It matters little that the shoneen Irishman announces that nothing is worth while writing except in the English tongue and much less does it matter that either the native Irish-speaker or those who have had to learn their Irish should say that my Irish is that of the Pale. I am very proud of the Dublin Irish. God bless the Dubliners! If the native language is ever to be revived as the common language of the country, it will be the people of Dublin who will be responsible for it just as they were behind everything else that was to the benefit of Ireland. Do not say that such talk is Provincialism or Metropolitan and anyone who knows what a Dubliner is will understand the truth of my saying. Many an Irishman born far away from the capital has been nurtured in mind and moulded in thought there, and in its surroundings has learnt the priceless truth that to lose one's earthly possessions in a noble cause is a thing worthwhile. For all that I may have to turn to the English at times in order to explain more clearly what I have in mind.

I hesitate to write the events of my life as I am not a person who performed any heroic deed. But as I happened to partake from beginning to end in the battle against the British Empire and as I happened to know most of the illustrious men and women who figured in the national movement, it would appear that I have knowledge of things and events which are worthwhile recalling, especially if others write down what they know and so enable someone in time to come to compare our statements.

As far back as my memory brings me that ideal known as the 'Fenian Faith' (or the Separatist Spirit) was embedded deeply in my heart. I inherited it from my ancestors and during my childhood and my youth things happened which fostered that faith, things which would seem to others at first sight, to be of trivial importance. I was born in Dublin April 1886. My parents had eight children but the two eldest died young leaving me the eldest of those that lived.

My father was a Dublin man. He was the youngest of the family of Thomas Henderson, Master Saddler, who lived at 140 Stephen's Green West, Dublin City. My grandmother died in 1845 the year of my father's birth and my grandfather, Thomas Henderson died later in the same year. Robert was my father's name and he had a hard struggle for existence even though his father was quite prosperous at his death. My grandfather made an unusual will so that none of the family could claim his or her portion of the family inheritance but only the benefits ensuing from the treasury in which his or her shares were invested. My father was apprenticed to the Book-binding trade and by that trade he earned his living till his death on 14th January 1910. With the exception of one daughter, Mary Anne, the rest of my grandfather's family died before I was born (1886). My father and my aunt told me the history of their own ancestors — that their father's father was an Orangeman, that he had a high rank in the Orange Order, that he had connections with Co. Fermanagh, Belfast and Dublin, and that his portrait was kept in the home depicting him dressed up in the Orange regalia. Their own father, Thomas, whom I mentioned before was married to a lady of the old Huguenot stock from Dublin. Her surname was Purdue (Barbour is what my brother Leo says it was, but I think Barbour was a relative of hers, or perhaps he was a barber). They had six children. Thomas Henderson was a Protestant Orangeman when he married, but sometime after his marriage, he became a Catholic and from what I gathered from my father, Thomas also at this time sided with the National movement which was in swing at the time and he had advanced views on the subject. His wife never became a Catholic but rather did she vehemently oppose the upbringing of the children in the Catholic Faith. Anyone intimate with the history of the Huguenots will understand her attitude and how bitter she could be in that line. Anyhow all the children were brought up in the Catholic Faith. Thomas Henderson (and his wife also I think) was buried in St Paul's graveyard, North King Street, Dublin. This is a Protestant Churchyard in which Thomas's relatives were buried before him.

As I said there were six children in Thomas's family, two sons and four daughters. The eldest was called William or 'Bill' and he was many years senior to my own father Robert who was the youngest. Uncle Bill was often said to be a bit wild or feather-headed. At any rate he joined the Fenians and like many other of his comrades he joined the British Army in order to learn the art of soldiery. He seems to have had a high rank in the Fenians as we were told that he was sent to America on some mission but that he failed to reach that country as the British arrested him on board a ship at Liverpool. He had left the barracks in which his battalion was stationed (Preston I think) in civilian clothes. At this time his sisters and possibly my father were residing in Manchester. He was brought before a military tribunal, court-martialled and deported to India where he died a while afterwards. It is not known whether this occurred before or after the rescue of the Fenians from the police van in Manchester 1867.

When my father finished his apprenticeship at Book-binding about 1866 he went to Manchester to seek for work and there he remained mostly up till the year he married, Christmas 1882. I could never make out for certain whether he ever entered the Fenians. He told me he was in Manchester at the time of the attack on the police van which freed the Fenian officers and oftentimes as a young lad he told me intimate things dealing with that rescue which only one who was in the Fenians could know or at least one who took special interest in the cause of the Irish at that period. Many years afterwards between 1904–1909 I got to know many of my father's old friends in Manchester when I went there on holidays and it surprised me what little regard they had for the Irish Parliamentary Party and how enthusiastic they were over the Gaelic League and the new Sinn Féin movement. I had a strong notion that they were old Fenians but whenever I tried to entice them to talk about the events of 1867 they always closed up.

It was from my father that I first heard of Brian Boru, the coming of the foreigner to Ireland and his subsequent suppression of the Gael, the efforts made from time to time to shake off the imperial yoke and especially of the 1798 Rebellion and the leaders connected with it, such as Lord Edward FitzGerald, Wolfe Tone, Michael Dwyer. He was greatly opposed to Parnell since the split among the Irish after the case of Kitty O'Shea had come before the Courts. I was five years of age when Parnell was buried and there was a public funeral on a Sunday in the beginning of October 1891. My mother thought highly of Parnell for all he had done for Ireland and yet my father refused to accompany her to the funeral. It was left to myself to stay at home with my father or go with my mother to Parnell's funeral and seeing that the public had such a regard for Parnell (although I could not understand what it meant) I decided to go with my mother. For a long time I thought it was because of the shameful affairs related between Parnell and Mrs O'Shea that my father disliked him so much, as my father was a very pious man and had sought admission to the Franciscans in his youth but was refused owing to bad health. But later I began to realise that that was not the full reason and that the old Fenian faith in him had much to do with his dislike for him as well. Whatever may have been the reason when the 1798 centenary celebrations took place in 1898 my father was as enthusiastic as any other separatist who was growing up and he took part whole-heartedly in the procession around the city on the Sunday on which the foundation stone of the memorial to Wolfe Tone was laid at the junction between Grafton Street and Stephen's Green, a few score yards from the house of my father's birth. He took myself and my brother Robert with him on that occasion and I well recall the huge crowd and their great excitement.

When England declared war on the Boers in South Africa in 1899 he openly deplored England's act. The day that Kruger the Boer General was forced to surrender after a fierce fight and being surrounded on all sides by the enemy, my father was so upset that one would think he had suffered a personal calamity. After that he sided much with John Redmond, Leader of the Irish Party in the House of Commons and he would advise me not to have anything to do with the advocates of physical force or with secret societies. 'Look at your Uncle Bill', he would say, 'whom nothing would satisfy but bloodshed, and yet he died over there in India oppressing the people of that country for John Bull.' 'And what happened eventually to the fine Fenian movement but the members going to the dogs, drinking, breaking up into splinter groups so that in the end the gun-drilling they had practised for so long was directed against each other.' He had seen such corruption and degradation after the defeat of 1867, the founding of the 'Invincibles', their collapse, the Parnell split and the death of the Chief that he lost hope in the success of the fight for Irish freedom through physical force.

My mother's people heralded from the North though she herself was born in Manchester 1860. Frances Broughal was her maiden name and she was fifteen years younger than my father. Her parents were James Broughal from Co. Armagh and Bridget Kearney (or Carney) from Newry and she was the only child. Her father was a dyer and he was quite prosperous until one 12th July when the Orangemen plundered his mill in Newry because (as we were told) himself and his people had openly sided with the National movement in the North. I believe he did not do so well in Manchester and he had to seek employment in some of the cotton warehouses. I never saw him. He died in Manchester a few years after my mother's marriage. My mother received a good education and she was a teacher in a Catholic school in Manchester when she married and then came to live in Dublin with my father. When I was ten years old an aunt of my mother's — Anne Broughal — came to live with us from Manchester and it was with us she died a few years afterwards. She had Irish and she would say the prayers in Irish with me when I began to ask her questions about the language. Both from her and from my mother I found out that their people had always taken part in the efforts to regain Irish freedom and that they suffered and lost quite a good deal in the service of such a cause. It was traditional among my mother's people that their forefathers had fought in the 1798 Rebellion and that even before that period they had taken part in any movement or society founded for the purpose of restoring to Ireland her long lost freedom either by force of arms or by whatever means were most effective at the time. Anne Broughal told me that one time she was ashamed of her life when as a young girl her brothers tried to interrupt Daniel O'Connell and he holding forth at one of his monster meetings. Although she could not understand why they should interfere with such a man as O'Connell I myself understood even though I was very young when she told me. I gathered from the stories she told me of that period that there was a group of young Irishmen in the country who were by no means satisfied with O'Connell's methods for restoring their rights to the Irish people and who thought that no means but those of physical force were of any use.

I have little knowledge about the Kearneys (or Carneys) but as far as I could gather they left Newry to go to Manchester. They were men of fine tall athletic physique and they joined the Fenians at their inception. One of their stock was Hugh Kearney — a blacksmith, a hurler, an athlete, a weight-thrower and a sweet singer. He used to sing in the Church of the Holy Name in Manchester.

How long-winded this is! I had to prove somehow that I inherited the Fenian faith from my fore-fathers, especially as the name Henderson is not an Irish one. I suppose my ancestors originally came from the Scottish Highlands to help the English to oppress the Irish!

And now I will begin my life story proper.

I first went to school at the age of five [in 1891] to the Christian Brothers, St Joseph's, Fairview. At that time Parnell was the talk of the land. There used to be some talk also about the Fenians but all I understood from it was that they were a crowd who had failed and few praised them. There was much more talk and praise of '98 and the people of that period. I was very friendly with a boy who lived near us called Walter Carraher. We went to school together. He hailed from Wexford and never ceased telling me about the heroic deeds of his country men in 1798. Between what he told and what I learned from my father regarding the men who fought in Dublin in 1798 there was enkindled in my young heart a strong desire to strike a blow for the freedom of Ireland some day. Walter died at the age of nineteen. Strange though it seems but his father, his grandfather, his brothers and some of his uncles were in the British Navy. Walter himself was trying to go there too before he took up printing. His uncles who were not in the Navy were members of the IRB and could be seen playing hurling at a time when that game was looked upon with contempt in Dublin. They belonged to a team called 'Brian Boru's'. Patsy Devlin ('Celt') was with them also. It appears that Walter's people lived by the Wexford coast and for generations back the men had always gone to sea and at that time it was difficult for them to become skilled sailors without joining the British Navy.

I was not long at school when there occurred an incident which has never left my memory. A brother called Mescall (God rest his soul) was teaching us grammar. He was using a book with questions and answers called the 'Expositor'. He explained to us the answer to the first question 'What is grammar?' The next question 'What is English grammar?' he explained as the 'art of speaking and writing the English language correctly'. When he had explained this he closed the book and quietly addressed us in solemn tones 'Are you English boys?', 'Why do we speak the English language?', 'Is there an Irish language?' Then he told us that there was an Irish language and what had happened to it. He must have spoken from the depths of his heart for he held us all spellbound. From that on I was always anxious to learn Irish and I had my father bothered with it as he had not a word of it in his head till I began to learn it in the same school 1899

It was Bro. Costen who first taught us the language. He was a Corkman and I think a native Irish-speaker but I don't think he had the proper books, Joyce's Grammar etc. However he did his level best. He was a friend of Fr Hickey and he was sent to Rome to take over a Christian Bros School there. After a while we were very lucky to get Bro. Casey as teacher. He was on fire with love for Irish and besides having learnt it minutely he also had a grand method of teaching it. He was a fine character and an excellent teacher. It was a cause of bitter disappointment to many of his past-pupils that he left the Order owing to a dispute between himself and his Superiors. The saddest part of all was that this rupture came about partly on account of either the revival of Irish or the method of teaching it and the question of authority in the Order.

Shortly after I had begun to learn Irish a branch of the Gaelic League was founded in Clontarf. The classes were first held in the Brothers' school at Marino and later in the National School at Philipsburgh Avenue, Fairview. Among those on the Committee of this branch were Thomas O'Neill Russell[2] — a well-known Irish scholar — and Willie Rooney.[3] A short while after the founding of this branch Willie Rooney became ill and died of consumption. I only knew him a short while but I knew his people very well. A brother of his, Johnnie, took part in the 1916 Rising. I knew the father very well. 'Mr Rooney' we used to call him. He was an old Fenian and in my opinion a sincere and loyal Gael and a gentleman. He was a tall straight but quiet man with a beard. One would take him to be a character of Kickham's stories, Mrs Rooney herself was a grand gentle quiet and peaceful lady with a pleasant countenance. The death of William Rooney was a big loss to Ireland — a poet, and a writer, he was burning with zeal to see his country free and to see the native language restored. He was a man of great sincerity. He killed himself in his early life (28 yrs) working relentlessly at a time when the old movement for full freedom of the people and restoration of the language was being re-shaped and re-organised.

Thomas O'Neill Russell was the teacher in the branch but he was not successful in that line though he had fluent Irish. The branch did not last long. But some other Irish groups were formed in the neighbourhood, a branch of an Irish political movement for instance called 'Cumann na nGael' which was founded about this time and which lasted till the coming of Sinn Féin. From these groups there sprung up 'Clann na h-Éireann' in Fairview. The Irish language, Irish dancing, Irish History etc. were taught there. It was founded for the young people and was a success. They built a hall in a yard behind one of the houses in Richmond Road facing the Tolka Bridge at Ballybough. It was in this hall that the Volunteers for Clontarf and Drumcondra area assembled together when they were first started. Here they did quite a good deal of drilling until their numbers grew so large that they had to go to Fr Mathew Park, Philipsburgh Avenue a very short while before the Howth gun-running 1914. I believe this club of Clann na h-Éireann was one of the visible wings of the IRB.

When I left school in 1903 the people of Dublin held hurling and Gaelic-football in scorn and contempt. It was said that these games were very rough and dangerous. The only ones to play those games at that time were the country lads who came to live in the city. To tell the truth the boys of Dublin were terrified of their lives because of the stories they used to hear in connection with these games. As well as that there were many people opposed to them and who showed their dislike by casting insults on the games, and those who played them. Association Football (or soccer, as it is called) was most commonly played and at times a bit of Rugby. I had a great interest in soccer and played at left-full back for a school team. As a boy I was often unwell but once I began to play soccer I enjoyed the best of health and I proved quite well as a player. We were winning everything before us when some of us began to read the weekly papers — 'The United Irishman' (Arthur Griffith)[4] — 'The Leader' (D. P. Moran)[5] and 'An Claidheamh Solais' (Gaelic League). In these papers young Irishmen were urged not to play the British games. Some of us tried to form a Gaelic team but we failed. Then one night shortly after the All-Ireland between Kerry and Kildare I heard for the first time of the ban on foreign garrison games by the GAA. This dealt with either playing the British games or of being connected with them in any way and immediately I turned my back on Soccer and Rugby. But I played no other game till the hurling team of the Ard-Chraobh was founded around 1903. When this club fell through in 1909 I joined the St Laurence O'Toole Hurling Club of which many of my friends were members. About the ban it must be said here that the common opinion among Gaelic circles at the time was that young

Irish boys were inveigled into the British Army through these Soccer and Rugby clubs and that the spirit of shoneenism was fostered among them in the clubs. Even though these clubs contained very loyal Irishmen — as good as any true Gael — and even though a great number of the Dublin Brigade were soccer players and soccer followers yet for all that quite a large number of them were affected by the British outlook just as the GAA held. Without a doubt the young men of the GAA had a more Irish outlook than those of the Soccer clubs. But the principal point was the majority of the GAA clubs were IRB circles. Else the members of the GAA were brought under the influence of the National movement and were asked to join active organisations for the fostering of the national spirit. After a trial period during which they were under supervision those thought to be most suitable were sworn in as members of the IRB. It would not be fair for me to omit the fact that most of the young men of the GAA down the country were hundred per cent and ever eager to play a man's part for Ireland. Still at the same time I must admit that there was a lot of hypocrisy or lip-service about many of the GAA members in Dublin, both young and old, at the time. The people of Dublin have always been ready to challenge the oppression of the Empire on the field of battle or in any other field but one must remember that the population of the capital is made up of many sorts and none of these groups could say that they were better than others in the fight for freedom. All contained both good and bad.

There were three events which helped a great deal to focus the attention of the rising generation at this time on the dire state of their motherland: the Jubilee Anniversary celebrations in honour of Queen Victoria and her visit to Dublin in 1897;[6] the Centenary celebrations to commemorate the Rebellion of 1798 and the Boer War in South Africa 1899–1902. I became aware, even tho' I was very young, that there was a small faithful party there who caused derision and scorn to be cast at the shoneens who tried to welcome Queen Victoria to Dublin, and who were behind the demonstrations of protest in the streets of the city when those same shoneens were bent on showing their loyalty to the 'Famine Queen' to the world.

When the war between the Boers and the British began anybody who had any spark of nationality in him showed his opposition to England. The Irish Brigade was founded in South Africa to help the Boers and many of the Irish working there joined it as well as other Irishmen from Ireland and America. Among these was Major McBride[7] who was later executed in 1916 for his part in the Easter Rising.

I got on well at school and it was arranged for me that I would enter the civil service. Of course this was under the British government and when the time came for me to leave school I flatly refused to undergo an examination for same. This was a heavy blow to my parents who had spent a lot of money to provide me with a suitable education and had kept me at school till leaving age. A short while after I procured a job as an office clerk, King Edward VII of England paid a visit to Dublin and the bosses of the business to which my office belonged allowed us all out for a half-hour to see 'His Majesty'. I said I would prefer to remain at my work. Everyone said I was mad even those who were fanatical in their denouncement of England and who would curse herself and her Empire to the devil. Needless to say I did not do so well in that office afterwards.

During these years I managed to get a good grasp of the language, both in speaking and writing it even though Irish books were scarce and seldom would one have a chance to hear or hold a conversation in Irish with another Gaelgeoir. After doing his best for us at school the advice Br. Casey gave us was to continually read Irish without attempting to translate it into English and always to say the words to ourselves. He promised us that if we were patient with ourselves it would not be long till we would understand everything we read and besides, we would succeed in thinking in Irish after a short while. His word was true, at least it proved to be so in my own case. It thrilled me to the heart when I paid a visit to Omeath (Co. Down) in 1903 that I could understand the old native speakers there sufficiently well and when they spoke to us in Irish they were able to understand my Irish. The only fault they had to find with me was that I was a Munsterman! (or had a Munster *blas* or Munster Irish).

I joined the Ard-Chraobh (Highest Branch) of the Gaelic League in Autumn 1903 and I was not long attending the classes, lectures, etc., till I could say without exaggeration that I knew the language fluently. Above all else I benefited very much from the classes of Micheál Mac Ruaidhrí from Fo-Choill, Mayo, who had the richest of Irish. Micheál was Pádraig Pearse's gardener at St Enda's and though advanced in years he took part in the 1916 Rising.

Around 1908 or 1909 I spent my summer holidays at Inishmaan, the Aran Islands, and every summer till 1913 I spent a fortnight there. At that time a visitor crossing to Aran on the steamboat would have to spend the night beforehand in Galway city and rise early the next day to sail. 'An Dubhros' was the name of the boat at that time before the 'Dún Aengus' came along to replace it. It was a real tub, small, poky and old-fashioned. Many a bout of sea-sickness came upon me making the journey from Galway to Aran. At that period there were many train excursions from Dublin to Galway at 4/– and I would join them a few times a year. I would take a quick journey to Mionloch on Loch Corrib and to Spiddal, speaking Irish to the people of those towns. But when we had sufficient time it was to Aran we would go, as there was no beating Aran, especially Inishmaan as regards fluency of Irish speaking, hospitality and friendliness of the islanders, healthy food and cleanliness of the homes. They were a fine sturdy stock these same islanders — sincere, industrious, without duplicity or obstinacy but independent at the same time, with no time for snobbery or its followers but people with courtesy bred in them. It was a bitter disappointment to me when the World War began in 1914 and my means were not sufficient to allow me to travel to Inishmaan any more.

Shortly after I went to the Ard-Chraobh a hurling team bearing the same name was founded and I became a member of that club. This was the first time for me to handle a *camán* (hurley) and even though I never became as skilful a player at hurling as I was at soccer, I loved this ancient Irish game and nothing pleased me so much as to spend much of my holiday time hurling with the *sliotar*.

There were many hurling clubs in Dublin at that time and most of the members belonged also to the IRB (Irish Republican Brotherhood). To tell the truth most of the clubs sprang from the new national movement which was flowering at the time. What usually happened was that any suitable person who proved himself well at these hurling clubs — or any Gaelic club for that reason — was approached by a promoter of IRB with a view to becoming a member of the IRB.

Such was not so in my case and it is difficult for me to make out why not. One of those days a young man was accidentally wounded by a gun in a house in the city. Someone told me that the men involved were friends of his and that they were members of the IRB. I think he thought I was also a member. That was the first time I had actual proof that such a Brotherhood existed. Other times I understood from the careless talk of others that such a Brotherhood was very lively and active. However Séamas O'Connor was Captain of the Ard-Chraobh Hurling team and as I learnt later it fell to him to recruit members from this club for the IRB. Although we were great friends and I never kept my views private regarding the emancipation of Ireland from the Crown, yet he never approached me on the IRB question. This is harder to understand when I recall working very hard for a few years as Secretary to the hurling club and in the Irish classes. And all during this time I was fully aware that there were other activities afoot besides hurling, dances, language etc. by the members of these clubs. I have no explanation for it unless it be the leaning I had towards Socialism or the close friendship I had with a person who sided with John Redmond and the UIL [United Irish League].

About 1909 the Ard-Chraobh hurling club was disbanded and I joined the St Laurence O'Toole Club. I began to teach Irish there just as I was doing in the Ard-Chraobh for a number of years, and when some of the members of this latter club proposed to start a Pipers' Band I worked zealously for this objective. And at long last I was asked to join the IRB. It was Seán O'Casey,[8] dramatist, who composed 'Juno and the Paycock', etc. who approached me on the matter. After pondering over the question for a week I refused. I explained to him that I understood from the Pronouncement of the Bishops in their Pastorals on 'Secret

Societies' that they prohibited the IRB. Even though I had decided to take part in the Rising which I knew was to happen later and even though I did not know how such a Rising could be effective without some system such as the IRB, I could not reconcile the two viewpoints — the aim of the Brotherhood and the prohibition of the Church. I would be endangering my life in the cause and seeing that there was no turning back for me once I had taken the step this was a difficulty which I must solve beforehand. This whole question caused me intense anxiety for a long time. Yet I knew that there was a solution to this problem which would not be a problem later to others besides myself. Therefore when the Irish Volunteers were founded the mental agony over this question which had disturbed me disappeared. I well understood that the IRB were behind this new movement, but even if they were, they had now openly asked the young men of Ireland to unite together and to take their stand in the political life of the country and it was clear that by so doing there would come a time at a future date when a blow would be struck for Freedom. As far as the question affected me I never at any time believed that anybody had a right, be he clergy or layman, to dictate to the Irish people that they needed a warrant to shake off the yoke of the oppressor by force of arms or by any other means but for all that I was not satisfied that the clergy had not the right to tell the people that they could not bind themselves by oath to a secret society. When the Volunteers were founded in 1913 I did not dwell much on the question, indeed I was under the impression that from now on there would be one source of Authority i.e. the Volunteer organisation. This was my belief until I was approached a second time to join the IRB. It was Brian O'Higgins[9] who asked me this time and I was an officer or a sub-officer. He put forward many plausible excuses why I should consent to becoming a member and I admitted that they were very good reasons but the prohibition of the Bishops against secret societies was still there and I told him I would prefer to remain as I was, that I knew a blow would soon be struck for freedom, and that at any rate I thought at this stage that the IRB was superfluous in spite of the good reasons he forwarded for its existence. I held that the Volunteer movement was sufficient with its organisation and control. Before the Rising I knew that many of my colleagues in the Volunteers were also members of the IRB and some of them used to be enticing me into it. The question was frequently debated between Oscar Traynor and myself. I think my brother Leo was trying to coax me in too but 'not a budge nor the sign of a budge' would I give. After the Rising, about 1918, I was sworn into the Brotherhood, and I sought admission myself. But that is another story!

The description of those times would not be complete without a reference to the movement for the betterment of the workers of the country and the manner in which they vigorously protested against the oppression of the employers. Around the end of the last century and the beginning of the present there was a group in Dublin called 'The Irish Socialist Party'. Among the leaders were James Connolly[10] (1916 leader also) and William ('Bill') O'Brien.[11] James Connolly had gone to America before I began to get interested in them (1903 or so). They used to hold public meetings but little attention was paid to them. Much of their teaching and ideals appealed to me although I thought they were too much given to spouting long extracts from the International books of the Socialists and that they were leaning too much towards materialism. There is no doubt but that the common people were down-trodden at the time and under heavy oppression and there was no relief forthcoming but by uniting together and striking a blow against their bosses. Yet I was of the opinion that political freedom was a better objective and to break the connection with English rule in Ireland. Anyway after prowling around a while in their midst one of their members admitted to me that I could not be a Catholic and a Socialist at the same time. I had nothing more to do with them from that on although I held that the strong grip that the Capitalists had on the workers would have to be shaken. At the same time the spirit of impatience was rife among the young men and the Trade Unions were to the fore in this matter going from strength to strength.

Recollections of Frank Henderson

(2)
Statement submitted to the Bureau of Military History
1948

After the Split the Volunteer organisation had a weekly newspaper called the 'Irish Volunteer'. I think it was edited by John MacNeill[12] himself. It was very well written and I believe was responsible for attracting a number of new men into the Companies. The publicity from that newspaper and Pearse's[13] pamphlets succeeded in getting a number of new men into the movement and these were of a very good type. It was felt that these men could be depended on, because they knew what they were doing when they joined. Possibly a lot of them thought beforehand that it was all political bluff.

The arming went ahead. Small arms, including revolvers and a few automatics, were imported secretly and distributed. Rifles became available in different ways, sometimes by bribing soldiers in barracks. Arms and military equipment were also on sale to a limited extent at Lawlors, Fownes Street, and at Whelans, Upper Ormond Quay. Training was intensified, with plenty of route marching and manoeuvring in small parties across country.

Some time before the Rising, I cannot place the date but I suppose it would be about six months before the Rising, the Irish Volunteers held a recruiting campaign to offset the recruiting campaign of the British. The Volunteer recruiting campaign was a remarkable success. The man who stood out most prominently in that campaign was Thomas MacDonagh.[14] Some of the Unionist and pro-British papers said at the time that if they had a public speaker like MacDonagh on their side they would have thousands of young Irishmen in the British Army. This campaign strengthened our forces greatly. Some of the men who had taken the Redmond side at the Split returned to us.

Some time in 1915 I was elected Captain of 'F' Company, when M. W. O'Reilly, Captain following the Split, was transferred to the Brigade Staff as, I think, Assistant Brigade Adjutant. Owing to the fact that I was not a member of the IRB there was a delay on the part of GHQ in appointing the date of the election for Company Captain, as it was anticipated that the members would elect me. Oscar Traynor was elected 1st Lieutenant, and Patrick Sweeney, now deceased, 2nd Lieutenant. Sweeney had been QM before he was appointed 2nd Lieutenant, and he continued to do a good deal of QM's work. Amongst the NCOs we had Harry Colley, I think he was Company Adjutant at the time of the Rising, Major Charlie Saurin, Arthur Shields of the Abbey Theatre, and John Ward. The late Harry Boland[15] was a member of 'F' Company.

That brings us up to the end of 1915, and we intensified our drilling, marching and had lectures in the Company. Our officers were trained along with the other officers of the Brigade. Lectures were held every week at Brigade Headquarters, generally on a Saturday night. Brigade Headquarters was first in Kildare Street, for some time in Pearse Street (opposite Tara Street) and afterwards at No. 2 Dawson Street. We were lectured there by Pearse, MacDonagh, our own Commandant, Ceannt,[16] Major John MacBride and Monteith,[17] who was a 1st Battalion instructor and officer. James Connolly also lectured us on Street Fighting, of which it was said he had had experience in Mexico. He held that the British would never use artillery against the buildings in the city owing to the amount of English money invested in such property. As far as I can remember everybody going to those lectures was armed with a revolver; it was quite common to come armed to the Volunteer parades. Amongst the men who attended those lectures were Dick McKee,[18] afterwards OC of the Brigade, and Peadar Clancy.[19]

At these meetings the officers were gradually brought to the realisation that there would be a rising soon, without being told so in actual words. It was the preparation of minds more than anything else. Discipline was emphasised at almost every meeting, and the importance of the closed mouth was very successfully instilled into the men. An example of this is the fact that two officers who attended these meetings were punished for breaches of discipline. They were reduced in rank for the time being. Their rank was restored with great ceremony by Thomas MacDonagh a week or two before the Rising. This is to emphasise what the discipline was like. In my opinion the discipline was marvellous.

There were other meetings of officers besides the Saturday night meetings. There was one about three months before the Rising, which I think must have been a meeting of the Second Battalion officers because it was presided over by Thomas MacDonagh. I was there, my brother Leo Henderson was there, Oscar Traynor and others whose names I cannot now remember were there. At that meeting Thomas MacDonagh told us definitely that there was going to be a Rising. He did not say when, but he said it would be in the near future. He told us it would be an all-Ireland Rising, that we would not win, but that we would keep fighting the British for so long that we would attract world-wide attention. He said the fight would start in the cities, that as far as we were concerned it would be in Dublin, that after about a week's time we would be driven out of the city and we would take to the country, where we would put up a great fight for some time, but that eventually we would have to capitulate. MacDonagh also told us that this would be followed later by another fight, in which we would not be successful but would be nearly successful and from which we would get the greater part of what we were seeking. They were prophetic words. MacDonagh said that the first fight would stir the young men who were not with us yet, and that we would have a fight in which practically the whole country would take part, that the whole country would rise the second time and it would be a fight of a different nature. As it turned out the second fight did not take place as soon after the first as he appeared to me to think, although, of course, preparations began immediately the survivors were able to pick up the threads of organisation.

There was another meeting at No. 2 Dawson Street on a Saturday night about a couple of weeks, at the most three weeks, before the Rising. I think every officer of the Dublin Brigade was present at that meeting. Some of the men at the meeting were in uniform and some were not. We were addressed, as well as I can remember, by Eamonn Ceannt who spoke to us about preparations for battle. MacDonagh also spoke as well as Ceannt, because I think both of them mentioned what they had done. For example, they said they had provided themselves with raincoats, leggings and marching boots. Ceannt mentioned that he had made his Will. There was a short pause, Pearse came in, and, after a dramatic silence of a few moments while he stood with his head down, he raised his head quickly and said, 'Is every man here prepared to meet his God?' He said it not loudly but with the force of tremendous seriousness. After that, Pearse proceeded to tell us that any man who was not in earnest now was his time to get out. Only a very small number, one or two men, did not turn up after that. Pearse said more, but that is all I can remember.

As regards the defence of meetings, the Headquarters staff themselves used to meet weekly, I think on Wednesday nights. Men were detailed at these meetings to guard against surprise, and cordons were thrown out to the different police barracks and to Dublin Castle, with a system of relays so that word could be got to Headquarters if any unusual activity was observed. These men were armed with revolvers. I was made Battalion Scout Commander, and I think it was by virtue of that position that I had charge of this business. I find from my notes that I used to have men from 'E' and 'F' Companies in turn, and perhaps sometimes together. I find also from my notes that this duty commenced on Wednesday, 25th August, 1915, and was continued on every Wednesday evening for some time. I do not know what date it was discontinued, but it went on up to fairly close to the Rising. I think that a similar system was followed for the meetings of officers.

In the meantime raids for arms and explosives were being carried out by the Volunteers. There was a notable raid on the London North Western Railway at the North Wall, which was conducted personally, I think, by Captain Weafer of 'E' Company. I knew about the raid but I was not on it. They got a number of British military rifles. Small quantities of explosives were got in some other places.

On Whit Sunday, 1915, there was a train excursion to Limerick on which the Dublin Companies went down with arms and ammunition, and those who had uniforms wore them. Each Volunteer paid his own fare. We had a recruiting march around Limerick and we marched through Irishtown. At that time a lot of the men from there were serving in the British forces and we had a very hostile reception. We had all sorts of missiles thrown at us. Not alone were Volunteers from Dublin on that excursion, but there were also Volunteers from Tipperary and

Limerick Counties, and I think from Cork and Kerry, taking part in it. There was a Company from Galbally and a Company from Ballylanders; they were strongholds of the Irish Volunteers. During the march some women ran in and tried to tear the uniforms off the men, some spat in their faces. We managed to keep our ranks, but the trouble started again when we re-formed to go home, and sticks and stones were produced. Some of the Redemptorist priests came along, got up on some prominent places and appealed to the crowd not to have bloodshed. We got away eventually, and only a few men were hurt. We had very strict orders that we should not injure anybody, because if we did it would only do harm to our cause. We got back to Dublin safely without further incident.

On a Saturday night in February, 1916, there was a raid for arms by the police in Great Brunswick Street, now Pearse Street. The raid was on the house of the FitzGeralds, who were prominent Volunteers in the 3rd Battalion. There were orders at the time that we were to defend our arms in our homes, and the FitzGeralds would not admit the police. Word was got around and the mobilisation of the Brigade took place. The 2nd Battalion mobilised around Ballybough; all arms and ammunition were brought out and it looked for a while as if the Rising was going to take place that night. Men were prepared for it, and not alone arms and ammunition, but military equipment of all sorts was brought out, and we waited in disciplined groups in the streets at Fairview and Ballybough, the other Battalions in their own areas. I suppose we must have been a couple of hours on the streets. I do not know whether the police went away or not, but in any case we got the order to dismiss. The men were told that night to be prepared for anything, and I believe, from what I heard afterwards, that the event very nearly precipitated the Rising. That was a great test of the men themselves, because there was always the doubt before that as to how many men would turn out when it would come to the point.

Another event was the review in College Green on St Patrick's Day, 1916, when Eoin MacNeill, who was Chief of Staff, took the salute. All the Companies of the Dublin Brigade took part in it and it was a great success. All traffic was held up for a few hours. The men were well drilled, and were what we at the time thought well armed. This review hardened discipline, strengthened the spirit of the Volunteers, and also got us some recruits.

One incident, which is worth recording, took place during that review. Some British military officers coming from the Castle tried to get through. The 3rd Battalion was at the flank nearest the Castle, where the Military officers came and were held up by the 3rd Battalion in charge of Eamon de Valera.[20] The British officers insisted that they would not be turned aside, but Eamon de Valera was just as insistent that they would not get through. It looked for some time as if it was going to be nasty. De Valera said he would use force, if necessary, and eventually the officers thought better of it and went off.

The actual review was preceded by a march around town. I was in charge of 'F' Company, and we numbered forty-four men there that day. We had been left with about forty men at the time of the Split and it fell away after that, so we were delighted to get forty-four out on that parade. The number of men of 'F' Company who went into action in Easter Week was 65. About half were in the GPO area and the other half in Jacob's area.[21]

The Rising

Large scale manoeuvres were notified to the Volunteers for some time previous to Easter Week, 1916. The people were used to seeing men going around carrying arms in military formation, and carrying out manoeuvres even in the city, so that nobody took any notice after a while.

In connection with these manoeuvres it was notified that they were to be on a larger scale than usual; that all arms, ammunition and equipment were to be carried; that men who had not been in the habit of parading openly with their Companies, such as Civil Servants, men employed by such firms as Guinness's who might be victimised, would be mobilised.

These men would not march with their Companies but would keep near them on the footpath and their arms would be carried by other members of the Company. The orders were to carry several days' rations, I do not know whether the number of days was specified. The officers of 'F' Company, probably on the recommendation of Thomas MacDonagh, decided to issue printed mobilisation slips on this occasion.

The mobilisation order was issued about a fortnight before the Rising. The word of the mobilisation came gradually, it was just mentioned, and then more about it the following week in greater detail. That brought us up to Holy Week, and during that week the Companies of the 2nd Battalion were paraded in strength on their parade nights in Father Mathew Park. 'C' Company, however, may have been paraded in their usual hall in 25 Parnell Square. Each Company in turn was addressed by Thomas MacDonagh on the different parade nights. In these addresses, which were very impressive, MacDonagh did not actually say that there was going to be a fight, but I do not think anybody was left under any misunderstanding. Each of these addresses was like the final exhortation of a General to his troops before going into battle. MacDonagh gave no direct indication that there was going to be a Rising, but most of the men guessed from what he said that it was coming off. The officers who were members of the IRB probably knew definitely that it was coming off. I knew, although I was not told directly and I was not a member of the IRB at the time.

The Companies of the 2nd Battalion at that time were 'B', 'C', 'E', 'F', and 'G' Companies. There was also probably a 'D' Company, consisting of men who were on night work and men like grocers' assistants who would be working late and who could only come on parade on Sunday mornings, but whether it actually existed at the time of the Rising or not I do not know for sure. My impression is that there was a Company which embraced such men in the 1st and 2nd Battalions. Men like Paddy Moran,[22] who was afterwards hanged, and Martin Savage[23] belonged to it. After the Rising it was formally known as 'D' Company of the 2nd Battalion, but beforehand it seemed to embrace both the 1st and the 2nd Battalions.

During Holy Week stores of ammunition and equipment began to be kept in the pavilion in the Father Mathew Park, and during the latter end of the week there were all-night armed guards on these stores.

As far as I know there is not much known about the original plans for Easter Week. I was told after the Rising by Dick McKee, later OC of the Dublin Brigade, that he was to have seized Trinity College with his Company. He was in charge of 'G' Company, and he was to have established communication with the 3rd Battalion through Lincoln Place and Westland Row, and that I, with 'F' Company, was to have seized the Bank of Ireland. We would then dominate that portion of the city and the approaches towards the centre from Dublin Castle. I have an impression that Dick McKee knew of those plans from Thomas MacDonagh.

It might be no harm to mention at this stage that after one of the parades in Father Mathew Park during Holy Week, Thomas MacDonagh asked me if I would accompany him when he was leaving as he wanted to have a chat with me. I was very busy with Company work on that particular night, probably Holy Thursday night, and I asked him if he could excuse me as I had a couple of hours of Company work to do at the time. He did excuse me, saying that he would see me again. He was probably going to tell me of my part in the plans then. I have always regretted not going with him as that was the last time I saw him.

Good Friday was a Bank Holiday. Most of the men were not working and there was great activity in Father Mathew Park, the completion of all Company arrangements for the manoeuvres.

On Good Friday evening I heard that a vessel bearing arms, the 'Aud', had been captured somewhere on the South coast. I heard that from my brother Leo, he was in the IRB and I was not. I think the IRB officers knew a good deal about it. There was also something published in the evening papers,[24] I think on Friday, about a stranger having landed on the coast of Kerry and having been brought a prisoner to Dublin. It was rumoured that this stranger was Casement.[25] This may have been Holy Saturday, but I am practically certain it was Good Friday. I heard about the arms ship on Friday and I feel almost certain that I heard about Casement's capture on Friday also from my brother Leo. I was very enthusiastic on Friday until I heard of Casement's capture, the sinking of the 'Aud', and later the mishap to the men at Ballykissane Pier, Killorglin, who had gone to meet Casement, and it seemed to me then that we were going to have a repetition of all the previous insurrections. I should also mention that Michael O'Hanrahan,[26] who was QM either of the Battalion or of the Brigade — his actual position has been disputed — was in our house, which adjoined Father Mathew Park, at about seven o'clock on Good Friday evening. He had come to see my brother Leo. I knew O'Hanrahan very well and I said to him as he was going away, 'Well, Michael, are we going out on Sunday and not coming back again?' He answered, 'Yes, we are going out, and not coming back.'

On Saturday preparations continued in Father Mathew Park. The printed mobilisation slips were filled in by Lieutenant Oscar Traynor, who, I think, had printed them, and myself that evening, and were given to the men responsible for distributing them. We spent a good part of that Saturday afternoon making sure that we were leaving none of the Company roll out of the mobilisation. We completed our arrangements then about getting our ammunition and equipment into the Park, as well as collecting the rifles and ammunition of men who had been excused drilling, such as Civil Servants and others in certain business houses which were hostile.

The Captain of 'B' Company was Peadar O'Reilly, who was a delicate man. We got word on Saturday that he got a haemorrhage of the lungs, and Leo Henderson, who was Lieutenant, was appointed Captain. O'Reilly was brought to the Mater Hospital. The other officers of 'B' Company were Paddy Daly[27] and Michael Murphy. Eamon ('Bob') Price[28] was Captain of 'C' Company; Thomas Weafer was Captain of 'E' Company, and Dick McKee was Captain of 'G' Company. Captain Liam Breen was one of the Brigade engineering officers, as also was Liam Daly of Phibsboro', not to be confused with another Liam Daly in 'E' Company. Our Battalion first-aid officer was J. J. Doyle. Thomas MacDonagh was a member of GHQ Staff, he was in charge of the 2nd Battalion for the Rising, and Tom Hunter was Vice Commandant of the 2nd Battalion. A good many of the orders came from Hunter on account of MacDonagh's position. Tom Slator was probably Adjutant of the 2nd Battalion.

The 1st Lieutenant of 'F' Company was Oscar Traynor. Patrick E. Sweeney was 2nd Lieutenant. I am not sure who was Adjutant, I think it was Harry Colley but I am not sure. Colley was Assistant Adjutant of the Brigade afterwards. Our QM was Patrick (?) Breen, who did not turn out. Charlie Saurin was an NCO in the Company at the time. Captain M. W. O'Reilly had gone from 'F' Company to the Brigade Staff about a year before the Rising. The man who acted as 'Pivot' in the mobilisation scheme in 'F' Company was Sergeant John McQuaid. He afterwards joined the British Army owing to difficulties at home following the Rising. He had been a splendid Volunteer.

In the original mobilisation scheme for the Rising we were to mobilise at Beresford Place. The 2nd Battalion were to march from there to St Stephen's Green. Thomas MacDonagh had told us that we would be mobilised under the protection of the arms of a friendly army, meaning the Irish Citizen Army. The details of the mobilisation are subject to verification by other people who might remember more, but my recollection is that we were to march across to St Stephen's Green after mobilising at Beresford Place after dinner on Easter Sunday.

I had been at eight o'clock Mass on Easter Sunday morning, and was having my breakfast when a knock came to the door and a member of the Company, Conway McGinn, came in, produced the 'Sunday Independent', and said 'Have you seen this?', showing me the communication which MacNeill had sent to the paper calling off the parade.[29] After that, to the best of my recollection, a letter came from a friendly local priest drawing attention to MacNeill's order and asking us to obey it.

Some time after, as we were wondering what was going to happen, an order came from our Battalion Headquarters telling us that the manoeuvres were off temporarily, but that all Volunteers were to 'stand to arms' and on no account was any man to leave the city. I think that order was a written order. Although MacNeill was Chief of Staff there was no confusion as to what order was to be obeyed, because we were in the habit of receiving orders through our own immediate superior officers. This bears out what I have already said about discipline. Everybody was wondering by this time what was going to happen, because MacNeill was a much respected man. The order to 'stand to arms' was conveyed to everybody in the Company through the mobilisation scheme, and men were appointed to do guard duty over the Companies' equipment in the Father Mathew Park, with the usual reliefs. There was a large amount of ammunition and equipment belonging to the different Companies of the 2nd Battalion, and I think also a good deal of 1st Battalion and GHQ equipment, possibly some explosives and electrical equipment stored in the pavilion and outhouses of the Father Mathew Park. That meant that they had to be guarded all night, and the police spies began to be very active that Sunday night while our men were on guard. There was a lot of noise with both sides tramping about, and I got very little sleep that night. I was just beginning to get to sleep between six and seven o'clock in the morning when a message came to me from Tom Hunter, Vice Commandant, asking me to provide him with a number of cyclists, I think he said at ten o'clock that morning. I do not remember what number he wanted, probably eight or nine. I sent back word to Hunter that I was unable to provide him with the men because we had only a couple of cyclists in our Company. I did not attach any importance to that message, I thought it was merely routine, and went off to sleep.[30]

A further order came from Hunter at about nine o'clock while I was still in bed, to the effect that the Company was to parade with all arms and equipment at St Stephen's Green at ten o'clock that morning. Tom Hunter must have delivered that message in person, or else he was very near to hand. I said to him as soon as I saw him, which was in a very short time, that it would be impossible to get the Company to Stephen's Green at ten o'clock, and his reply was, 'Do your best, and get as many men as you can.' There was no doubt then as to what was going to happen, and I proceeded to set the mobilisation scheme in motion. I had to go some distance to get the 'Pivot', but I relieved him of some of the work by calling on some of the men on my way to him. I saw McQuaid, the 'Pivot', and told him what I had done. I then went home to get ready myself. On my way home I passed Tom Clarke[31] at the Tolka Bridge at Ballybough. He was proceeding on foot towards the city.

McQuaid lived on the East Road, then commonly called the Wharf Road, just at the point where the Great Northern Railway crosses. Some of the men lived as far away as Dominick Street, others as far away as Goose Green and Dollymount.

As the men were being mobilised I got a written order from Paddy Daly, I think he was an officer in 'B' Company, probably one of the Lieutenants. The order said to give him one reliable man for a special job, and it was signed by James Connolly. This order was addressed to the Captain of 'F' Company, probably my name was on it, and it was nearly ten o'clock when I got it. The special job was the blowing up of the Magazine in the Park, and the man was to report to Garry Holohan, I cannot remember at what time. They were collecting men from different Companies to carry out this job. The order did not state what the special job was, but I had been told about it some time before by Lieutenant O. Traynor.

I immediately queried the order, and the words I used to Daly were, 'Who is James Connolly?' Daly got annoyed, and I reminded him of the warning that had been given to us by Commandant MacDonagh that we were only to take orders from our own superior officers. Daly then said to me, 'Look at the other side of the order', and on the other side of the order, which was written on a small single sheet of paper, was a note signed by MacDonagh himself instructing me to carry out any orders given to me by James Connolly. Volunteer Bob Gilligan was then assigned to the job and went off.[32]

A short time previous to handing Volunteer Gilligan to Paddy Daly I had a conference with Tom Hunter as to what the position was, and we decided that I would get half of the Company over to Stephen's Green right away, and keep the other men as they came along to guard the large amount of stores in Father Mathew Park.

About this time people whom we knew to hold important positions in the movement began to arrive and warn us about going out and taking part in something that was not authorised. I knew that the IRB was at the back of everything, and I knew that some of these people were important people in the IRB. Seán Lester[33] was one of the men who came along and told us that everything had gone wrong and warned us about taking part in carrying out the mobilisation order. Some of the people who were with Seán Lester told us that there had been some rioting in the town, and that the Irish Citizen Army only had gone into action. I did not know Lester, but I was told by some of the other officers present that the principal spokesman was Seán Lester, who was a reporter on the 'Evening Mail'.

This led to a conference of the officers who were present. These officers were: Captain Thomas Weafer, myself Captain Frank Henderson, Captain Leo Henderson, and Lieutenant Oscar Traynor. I had carried out Vice Commandant Hunter's orders to get about half the Company over to Stephen's Green, and they were gone by this time. Captain Weafer and Captain Leo Henderson had done the same in regard to their Companies.

There was a certain amount of indecision as to what was to be done. Lieutenant Traynor was the only one who was in favour of proceeding immediately into town. I knew I was the only officer present who was not a member of the IRB, and I felt myself in a rather difficult position. I said, 'This thing should be settled by an order from the senior officer present, and the senior officer is Captain Weafer.' That was accepted by everybody. Weafer took charge and stated that he would go and see James Connolly personally and get the position cleared, that in the meantime the Volunteers present were to demobilise in small groups and go to certain houses, about half a dozen men to each house. He got the addresses and other particulars of these local houses, which were spread over Fairview and Summerhill on the way to town. I myself went to the house of Volunteer Conroy in Richmond Cottages, Summerhill and in about half an hour an order came from Weafer to re-mobilise immediately. I cannot be sure what time of the day this order arrived, but I think it may have been before the GPO was taken and that it may have been in Liberty Hall that Weafer saw Connolly.

We re-mobilised as quickly as possible. Weafer told us that when we re-mobilised we were to proceed to town immediately. Whether it was to the GPO or to Liberty Hall we were to go I cannot remember at this stage.

Although I do not actually remember it, I am almost certain that a guard was posted over the stores, etc., in Father Mathew Park. A horse lorry had been commandeered to carry the heavy stuff to where we were going, and I am almost certain that it was previous to the temporary demobilisation. A difficulty arose about the driver, who got timid, and refused to drive the lorry. After we remobilised a man was got who was both willing and able to take charge of the vehicle.

A few men who had been present when the order for demobilisation was given did not report back. I do not think there would have been more than half a dozen such men, and in some cases the fact that they did not come back was probably due to the difficulty in getting in touch with them.

When we re-assembled, Captain Weafer proceeded to form the column for the march into the city. According to my estimate there would be from 80 to 100 men there. Captain Weafer took charge of the main body, with which was the horse lorry and the various stores. He had from 30 to 50 men in the main body.

The advance guard of about 25 men was in charge of Leo Henderson, Captain of 'B' Company, and the rearguard of about 25 men was in charge of myself.

The men in the column were not all from one Company. There were men from 'B', 'E' and 'F' Companies of the 2nd Battalion, and also some 1st Battalion men.

The men in the column were greatly heartened by the action of Father Walter McDonnell, a Curate in Fairview parish, who came into Father Mathew Park, heard Confessions, and gave his blessing to all present before we moved off.

During the time of the temporary demobilisation we noticed that there was a great stream of refugees coming out from the city. It was a very pitiful sight in many ways, because there were families carrying a few belongings, hastily put together. Many of them showed traces of terror. Some of these people gave us heartening news, saying that our people held the city and had already defeated the British in a couple of battles; others told us the direct opposite.

The column finally moved off, at, I think, about three o'clock in the afternoon, but I am not certain of the time.[34] We proceeded from Father Mathew Park down Philipsburgh Avenue, turned right at the junction with Fairview Strand, proceeded over the Tolka Bridge at Ballybough, and along Ballybough Road towards the canal bridge at Summerhill. When the rearguard, of which I was in charge, got on to Ballybough Road, the sound of rifle and machine gun firing was heard, faint at first and then becoming very loud as if it was in close proximity to us. When the rearguard reached the junction of Bayview Avenue with Ballybough Road, I noticed that there was a body of armed men in Bayview Avenue near the North Strand end. I did not know at the time who they were, but I found out afterwards that they were the advance guard who had been sent down that direction by Captain Weafer to engage a British column which was coming from a training camp at the Bull Island, Dollymount, towards the North Strand. Captain Weafer had got information about this British column from scouts. When Captain Weafer came very near the crown of the hill, formed by the bridge crossing the canal, he stopped suddenly and gave me the signal to retreat. I concluded that the British forces were coming along Summerhill and that we were about to be attacked from that direction.

I sent one of my men to Captain Weafer to ask him for further orders. In the meantime he signalled to me to retreat at the double.

After a short time the man I had sent to Captain Weafer came back and told me that my orders were to seize a position commanding the Tolka Bridge at Ballybough. I proceeded in the direction of the bridge at the double, midst the jeers of some people on the footpath that I was running away.

I was making up my mind what position I should seize, and, as I saw that Captain Weafer was retreating with the main body, I decided to cross the river and seize a house, part of which was occupied by Gilbeys, Ltd, as a shop and wine store. It was a two-storey house and was occupied as a residence by an old lady and her daughter, as well as by Gilbeys, Ltd. It had a good commanding position in regard to the Tolka Bridge, and there was a window on the Fairview side of it which commanded a view of the approach from Fairview, along Fairview Strand towards the bridge. I had noticed this house before, because we had been instructed to watch out for buildings with commanding positions.

We had to turn the old lady and her daughter out of the house,[35] and I immediately proceeded to sandbag the windows and to put the house into the best condition we could for defence. Meanwhile there had been very heavy firing fairly close to us, but we could see no British troops. By the time we had the house ready for defence and got our men in positions at the windows the firing had stopped. There was dead silence all around, and not a soul to be seen on the streets.

I tried to find out what the position was as regards Captain Weafer, but I could not see him or any of his men. I never saw him again. I learned afterwards from some of the men who were with Captain Weafer's part of the column, that three or four positions between North William Street and Clonliffe Road had been entered by his men, and that when he learned from his scouts that the British column coming from Dollymount had been beaten off and had retreated towards the North Wall, he himself with his men proceeded towards the city. I received no orders of communication from him after his order to seize a position commanding the Tolka Bridge.

I decided to stay where I was and get in communication with GHQ. After a while my brother, Leo Henderson, who had been in charge of the advance-guard, came along with his men. He told me that he had been to the GPO, that James Connolly had told him to come back and reinforce our garrison, and that I was to remain there until I got further orders.

Some little time after we had seized the house we were now in, we were rejoined by Oscar Traynor, who, during the time between the temporary demobilisation and the present time, had been to GHQ and to the Magazine Fort in the Phoenix Park. Oscar Traynor confirmed the order from James Connolly that we were to stay where we were until further orders reached us. He also told us that the GPO and all O'Connell Street, as well as some of the adjoining streets were in the possession of our forces. Also that Captain Weafer had arrived at the GPO, and that he had spoken to him at a barricade in Abbey Street, near the Abbey Theatre.

From time to time we were reinforced by men who had been unable to join their own Companies, but who had been told by people on the streets that there were Volunteers in Fairview. Some of these men were from the 1st Battalion, as well as from our own Battalion.

When it was clear that the intention of GHQ was that we were to remain in Fairview, I decided to occupy another house, so as to gain complete command of the bridge over the Tolka from the city. The house we decided on was Lambe's public house, which gave us a complete view of the approach to the bridge from the city, and also defended it from an approach from Drumcondra direction via Richmond Road. Lambe's was on the North-West side of Tolka Bridge, and Gilbey's on the North-East side. The two positions were about fifty yards apart.

We had now three officers in Gilbey's; myself, Oscar Traynor and Leo Henderson. After having a short conference we decided that the three officers would stay in Gilbey's, which, although it was the smaller building of the two we had seized, appeared to us to be a more important one on account of its position. I appointed Seán Russell,[36] who at the time was Adjutant of 'E' Company, in charge of the garrison in Lambe's public house.

We made out the general routine orders of sentries, and tried to arrange times for rest, and so on. We then proceeded to stock our position with food. The first thing we did was to send to a butcher in Fairview, opposite Philipsburgh Avenue, for fresh meat, for which we offered to pay. He refused to give the meat to our men, so we took it by force. We also held up a bread-cart, which, I think, belonged to the DBC [Dublin Bread Company]. We took what we considered was sufficient bread for the time being, and gave the man a receipt in the name of the Irish Republic. The driver of the bread-cart was friendly. We also filled all the available vessels with water. This was in accordance with the instructions we had received from time to time in regard to street fighting.

After a short time we learned that there was a force of men in occupation of the offices of the Wicklow Chemical Manure Company at the junction of North Strand Road and Poplar Row. That was on the city side of the Tolka and was about 200 to 250 yards from our position. We did not know who they were, but after some time we learned that they were mainly men from the Citizen Army, who had been sent there by James Connolly. This body was in charge of a man named Craven, whose Christian name I cannot remember. He was one of the men who came over from Liverpool. He went to America many years ago. The second in command appeared to be Vincent Poole, a member of the Citizen Army. This was told to me by some men of my Company who had not joined us up to this, and had reported to Craven when they found that he was in action, but who preferred to be with their own Company when they learned that we were at Ballybough. Amongst those who came to me from that position were Harry Colley and the late Harry Boland. I was very glad to get men like Harry Boland and Harry Colley. They were a great help to the men, both by force of example and by their cheerfulness.

During one of our conferences that first evening, I was questioned as to whether we had our line of retreat made out. This was a matter the importance of which was impressed frequently both on officers and men during our training in the period before the Rising. We had a general line of retreat made out, although it would be very difficult to say where we would eventually get to if we had to retreat from the position.

We sent frequent communications to Headquarters reporting on what was taking place, the number of men we had, and the measures we had taken to defend our position.

No incident of note occurred during the night. We could hear the firing going on in the city, but there was no action on our part at all.

The party under Captain Craven at the North Strand Road bridge over the Tolka had skirmishes with a party of British on the Great

Northern railway. The British were forming an armoured train, and the engine had been driven down along the line over the sloblands a few times, while they were equipping the armoured train. Some civilians were killed by fire from the British on the GNR.

Nothing further happened during the night.

On Tuesday morning we held up, searched and questioned several suspicious-looking people who were hanging about our position, but without any result.

We had scouts out at all times, and as there were rumours that the British were advancing from the North we had pushed these scouts out as far as Malahide on their bicycles. During the morning these scouts brought us word that British troops had arrived at Malahide; later that they had come as far as Howth Junction and had disentrained there. Later in the day we learned that two forces of British troops were advancing, one along the Malahide Road towards Fairview, and the other along the Swords Road towards Drumcondra.

The armoured train appeared to have gone up towards the North early on Tuesday, and, acting on GHQ orders, we attempted to blow up the GNR line at the sloblands with gelignite. There was only a small quantity of gelignite, and our men were inexperienced in the use of explosives, so we were not very successful. This attempt was made, as far as I can recollect, about midday on Tuesday.

Having thought this over again, I now feel that the attempt to blow up the GNR line was carried out by Craven and on Monday evening. The party he sent to do it included a couple of my own Company who rejoined me later and told me about the attempt. One of these was Harry Colley, who was badly torn by barbed wire at the railway line.

We kept GHQ informed of the movements of the British as our scouts reported. I think GHQ also had reports independent of us. I was aware that they got reports of the general movements of the British through a friendly telephone operator named Matt Costello, who was a member of 'B' Company. He was also in touch with us at Fairview on Monday and Tuesday. His reports were made under the name of 'Brian Boru'.

Later in the day we ourselves decided to attempt to blow up one of the Great Southern and Western railway bridges on Clonliffe Road, as this was an important line leading from the North Wall to Kingsbridge. We had no gelignite with us, but one of our men, Seumas Daly, who lived in Dollymount, had some dumped in his house. We sent out for the gelignite, but we did not get it in time as our orders to vacate the position came before it arrived.

At about six o'clock in the evening our scouts reported to us that we were almost within a pincers between two British forces, one of which had arrived at Drumcondra from Swords, and the other had arrived at or about the junction of Malahide Road with Clontarf Road. This latter body was said to be slowly proceeding towards Fairview.

We prepared for the defence of our position, and addressed our men, preparing them for the fight that appeared to be about to take place. They were all in the best of spirits, determined to do the best they could.

We dispatched a messenger to GHQ, informing them of the position. This messenger returned with a written dispatch from James Connolly, in which he congratulated us on the good work which we had done already, and ordering us, if we could possibly do it, to retire immediately on GHQ. From the wording of the dispatch, which I read to our men, I am sure that Connolly thought we would never reach the GPO. We had at the time about 66 men, all told, and there was also the force at the North Strand end under Captain Craven, which I think consisted of about 25 men. In the dispatch from James Connolly he made me responsible for conveying the order to Craven's force, who were to follow us to GHQ.

We formed up on the road outside Gilbey's, made sure that we had all our arms and ammunition, and marched off. I warned the men before they started that it was going to be a forced march.

When we crossed the river to the city side and were passing by the junction of Clonliffe Road with Ballybough Road, we could see the British troops forming up at the Drumcondra end of Clonliffe Road. Craven's men were at the time coming up from their position, and I sent word to him of the position of the British and told him to take all the care that he could in passing Clonliffe Road.

We were also told by our scouts that the British were in possession of Amiens Street railway station, and that snipers were in the tower of the station.

We had a fair number of rifles, shotguns and revolvers. The rifles were mostly British long Lee Enfields, a few of the short Lee Enfields, a few German Mausers, some Howth Mausers, and there was a fair amount of ammunition for them all.

The British did not fire on us from their position at the Drumcondra end of Clonliffe Road. This may have been due to the fact that we had a few prisoners who were dressed in British uniforms. I think the prisoners had been taken mostly by Craven's party, who picked them up around the place.

We proceeded along Ballybough Road. I marched at the head of the column, with Lieutenant Oscar Traynor on one side of me and Captain Leo Henderson on the other. As far as I can recollect Seán Russell was in the rear. We were preceded by scouts on bicycles. These were young boys who were able to get around without exciting suspicion, and they kept us informed of the best line of advance, which was straight along Summerhill and Parnell Street until we got to Cumberland Street. The scouts informed us as we were approaching Cumberland Street that the British were at the Parnell Monument, so we could not proceed any further along Parnell Street without being seen by them, as the road takes a bend just there. We accordingly turned left into Cumberland Street, then right into Waterford Street, and left into Marlborough Street. The danger point in Marlborough Street was the crossing over at Talbot Street, on account of the British forces being in the GNR station. However, we got across without any casualties, turned right into Sackville Place, at the O'Connell Street end of which we encountered the barricades which had been erected by the Republican forces.

Firing was coming into O'Connell Street, apparently from the Parnell Monument direction and from the O'Connell Bridge direction.

We halted when we came to the barricades. Oscar Traynor dashed across the road in a zig-zag fashion, reported our arrival and asked what we were to do. He returned with orders that we were to get across the road in small groups. We got across and under the portico of the GPO without casualty. On the way across I noticed barbed wire barricades at the Pillar. There was also an overturned tram-car serving as a barricade at North Earl Street. There were other barricades between Abbey Street and O'Connell Bridge.

When we arrived under the portico of the GPO where the front entrance then was, we were fired on by our own forces who were in possession of the Imperial Hotel over Clerys. This was apparently due to the fact that we still had prisoners in British uniforms, and these had to dash across the road, the same as ourselves, and some of the men who were at the windows assumed that the British were attacking. A few of our men were slightly injured, and some confusion ensued as some of our men replied, without waiting for an order, to the fire which was coming from the Imperial Hotel. At this point James Connolly rushed out of the GPO, stood out on the road, held out his arms and shouted to the men in the Imperial Hotel that we were friendly troops and not to fire any more. The firing then stopped.[37] I noticed that a couple of light cables of wire or rope stretched from the GPO to the Imperial Hotel; and that they were used for conveying communications in small cars or boxes to and fro. These continued in use until destroyed by enemy fire.

James Connolly was dressed in the dark green uniform of the Citizen Army, with, I think, slacks of the same colour, and he had the slouch hat of the Citizen Army, caught up at one side.

We then proceeded into the GPO where we were addressed by Pearse, who was also in uniform. Pearse stood up on a large table in the public hall of the GPO, congratulated us on what we had already done, and prepared us for what was to come. We were all very deeply moved by his address.[38]

We observed that the inside of the GPO was prepared in a military fashion for siege or attack, windows were sandbagged and men were in position at them. The Cumann na mBan had a field hospital in a room just off the main hall. GHQ officers appeared to be in consultation in the main hall, repairs and alterations to which had just been completed before the Rising.

Immediately outside the GPO there were barbed wire and other obstacles, placed so as to hold up any force that would attack the building. There were also Republican Police in front of the GPO. These were ordinary Volunteers who had just been given Military Police duties. I think some of them had some kind of batons but I am not quite sure. They had to question anybody coming in towards the entrance, and they were also to keep looters and inquisitive people away. They had to question anybody leaving the post office as well.

After Pearse's address he handed us over to James Connolly, who, he told us, would issue orders to us.

Connolly first sent some of our men across the road to reinforce the garrison in the Imperial Hotel. I think that only a small number of men went over, probably not more than ten or twelve.[39] Connolly then sent a party of about 22 men into the Metropole Hotel in charge of Lieutenant Oscar Traynor, and he ordered me to proceed with my brother Leo Henderson, and about 22 men to Henry Street. There were no Republican forces in Henry Street at that time. Our orders were to make entries at two different points into the buildings flanking the GPO, and to erect two barricades, one at the O'Connell Street side of Moore Street and the other at the far side of Moore Street. One entry was to be made at McDowell's jewellery shop and the other at Bewley's provision shop. McDowell's shop at that time would be where the GPO Arcade is now, and Bewley's would be about where Woolworth's is now. We were to enter these premises and make sure that any civilians who were in them were sent away. We were to put the buildings in a state of defence, and to bore through the walls, first to one another, then to the GPO, and then West towards Arnotts.

As we went round to Henry Street there was not any great firing in O'Connell Street, but we went round in single file, hugging the wall. It was comparatively safe then in O'Connell Street. When we got round into Henry Street there did not appear to be any danger from fire by the enemy.

Remembering my experience in Fairview, when we had to turn people out of the houses when seizing them, I was very glad to find that the places we were to seize in Henry Street had already been vacated, with the exception of Bewley's stores where there was a caretaker who was inclined to give a little trouble in the beginning, possibly from a sense of duty. At the same time he did not appear to be disposed to us, but he had no choice in the matter. It might be well to mention about Henry Street, that right opposite Moore Street was the Coliseum Theatre and from that point down to near Arnotts the upper portions of the houses were used as residential flats. I ordered my brother to take charge of the entry at McDowell's shop, and I remained at the Bewley's shop entry myself.

As soon as we made the entry, I detailed men to fill all available vessels with water, and to take up positions on the second storey and to break the windows on that storey. This was in accordance with the directions we had received during training.

I also sent a party of men out to collect all the food they could get in the provision shops in Henry Street. As Henry Street was a centre for provision shops we obtained all we wanted of food that would keep. We sent large supplies of it to the GPO, retaining enough for our own garrison's use.

We proceeded to raid stores in Henry Lane to get tools for boring through the walls of the houses. We got the necessary tools in some of the stores there. We also proceeded to erect the barricades ordered by James Connolly, and we had to use whatever was at hand. The barricade that I personally supervised was the one at the West side of Moore Street. There was a tailor's shop close by in which there was a very good stock of cloth, which we brought out in bales to form the foundation for the barricade. The mob was fairly thick around Moore Street and Henry Street, and they proceeded to run away with the bales of cloth as quickly as we put them in position. In order to try and stop this, I ordered shots to be fired over the heads of the mob, but they had by this time got so used to the shooting that they did not mind it. I then ordered the men with bayonets to fix bayonets and charge the crowd but on no account actually to use the bayonets. This had the desired effect.

The boring of the walls was started at the same time. Leo Henderson worked from his position towards the post office, and I worked from Bewley's towards him. As it was very urgent to effect a passage right through to the post office we worked at it all night. Our work was made very easy by the fact that we had five brothers named Ring, four of whom were carpenters. We also had a friend of theirs named James Hunter, who was experienced in building work, and he was a great help. Their services were invaluable for the boring, especially when we came to the Coliseum wall, which was unusually thick. Following the instructions which we had received during lectures, we staggered the breaches in the wall as far as possible. By Wednesday morning we had a passage made from Bewleys right through to the post office. We then proceeded in the other direction, towards Arnotts. However, before this passage was complete, some time during the night, I received an order to report to Pearse in the GPO.

Having reported progress, at which he seemed pleased, Pearse ordered me to take a party of men and erect barricades in Henry Place and Moore Lane, in order to hold up any attempt by the British to advance by the back lane from Parnell Street and Moore Street. We completed this work in the darkness of the night in deserted streets, and reported back when it was finished. That brings us to Wednesday morning.

We continued to work hard at the borings in the direction of Arnotts.

The mob, who appeared to be seized with looting madness, gave us a lot of trouble during the early part of the day, but when the firing began to increase as the day went on they began to ease off. There were some casualties amongst the looters.

The attitude of the civilians towards us was mixed. Some were very hostile and some were friendly. A milk-man brought us milk two or three times during the day. He came again on Thursday. He volunteered to do this and refused to accept any payment. After about midday on Thursday we saw him no more. It would not then have been possible for him to get near the place.

The front of the Coliseum Theatre commanded the approach via Moore Street from Parnell Street, and we took special care to have a constant look-out from the windows and to have men ready to deal with any situation that might arise there.

Later in the day, Henry Street seemed to be raked with machine gun fire from both ends. The firing appeared to come from the tower of Amiens Street railway station and from Capel Street. British snipers were also very busy from this on. We tried to locate them from the roofs of our own buildings, but I do not know that we were successful. There was apparently one stationed about McBirneys, and several times he very nearly inflicted casualties on us while we were on the roofs.

At this period many non-combatants were killed in Moore Street and Henry Street. Among these was the father of Eimar O'Duffy,[40] who apparently was running from Moore Street into Henry Street to escape fire from the direction of Parnell Street when he ran into a burst of machine gun fire. He died in the middle of the road, and was attended to spiritually by Father John Flanagan, who was attached to the Pro-Cathedral. Father Flanagan was later Canon Flanagan of Fairview. He was one of the bravest men I ever met. He attended Mr O'Duffy and others in the middle of the street while the firing was going on. He also came into the post office and gave spiritual aid to the men there.

During the afternoon James Connolly came to my position through the passage we had made via the walls, and ordered me to have ready for him in about five minutes' time eight or ten — I am not quite sure of the number now — of the best men that I had. He said that he was going to lead them down to Liffey Street to try to dislodge a British party who were reported to have occupied some buildings there, and to have cut off some men whom Connolly had sent down via Abbey Street. As many of the men under my command at this time were not of my own Company and were unknown to me, I could only afford to select half of the number required from the men I knew. The others whom I selected appeared to me to be the best of the strangers. I had in mind that although I was giving Connolly a party of men, I was still responsible for the defence of the buildings I was in. I told off these men, lined them up and explained to them what they were required to do, and went away to complete some other task.

When Connolly appeared again, half of the men I had selected were not to be found. Connolly angrily demanded of me why I had not obeyed his order. I explained to him that I did not know all the men under my command at the time, and that, bearing in mind my responsibility as regards the position I was in, I had given him as many of my own men as I could reasonably afford, which would be about half the number he had asked for. I told Connolly that I could depend absolutely on my own men, but that the others did not appear to be so well disciplined, and that I did not know what had happened to them. Connolly accepted my excuse, but ordered me to have the full number of men ready in about three minutes' time. I then selected men to replace the missing men, and everything was in order when Connolly came again.

Amongst the men of this party were Tom Ennis,[41] later Commandant of the 2nd Battalion and in charge of the burning of the Custom House; Seán Kerr,[42] a member of a well known Republican family in Liverpool; Patrick Shortis, who was killed in Moore Street at the time of the evacuation of the post office, and Patrick Lynch, who died last year. These were all first-class men.

With this party Connolly went out into Henry Street, while it was still under fire. He led the party in single file down to Liffey Street and seized some buildings there. He had some skirmishing with the enemy and was out all that night, returning the following morning via Abbey Street. I believe that Connolly succeeded in dislodging some party of the enemy and also in rescuing his own party who had been cut off. Amongst those in the party who were cut off was the late Seán Milroy.[43]

I later discovered the men who had been missing from my post, and spoke to them very severely about absenting themselves. Their action, I believe, was entirely due to lack of appreciation of discipline.

During this day, Wednesday, rumours were very prevalent that the Germans were in Dublin Bay and on the Naas Road; also that there had been big fights in the streets of Limerick, and that the Pope had sent His Blessing. In order to verify whether the account of the Germans being in Dublin Bay was correct or not, I took an early opportunity of going up on the roof of the post office, from which there was a splendid view over the Bay. However, I could see no ships of any kind in the Bay.

Our force in Henry Street, which had started at about twenty-two, was augmented from time to time by men sent from the GPO. I think about a dozen extra men, altogether, were sent.

During the evening I noticed that fatigue was beginning to tell on our men, and, as the interior line of communication to the GPO had been established, I arranged periods of off-duty to allow the men to rest. In order to show how fatigued our men were I may mention that I came upon one of the look-out men in the Coliseum, early on Thursday morning, standing in the window with his head resting on the outer sill, fast asleep.

Nothing of note took place during Wednesday night except that there was continuous rifle and machine gun fire. Several buildings had gone on fire at this time, both in O'Connell Street and further down towards Capel Street.

From the time we came into the buildings in Henry Street there were about half a dozen members of Cumann na mBan attached to us. They cooked our food and served it to us, and remained on the alert for any eventuality.

On Thursday we continued boring towards Liffey Street in compliance with our orders. By the afternoon we had arrived at the outer wall of Arnott's warehouse.

All day Thursday the sniping by the enemy was continuous. He appeared to be establishing himself more firmly in houses at the junction of Mary Street and Capel Street, from which point he poured heavy rifle and machine gun fire in our direction. During the day on Thursday a shell struck the GPO. This, I believe, came from the river, on which the British had the SS 'Helga', or it might possibly have come from a gun which the British planted at the Crampton Monument. This shell appeared to shake all the buildings. Meanwhile, the fires were spreading in the adjoining streets, probably the result of the firing of incendiary bombs by the British.

In reply to orders from the GPO, we sent to them further large quantities of food which we had seized from the shops in Henry Street. We, however, kept enough food for our portion of the garrison, and continued our arrangements to cook what we required for ourselves.

In the afternoon of Thursday, while boring through the walls close to Arnotts, we noticed that a British armoured car had come down Henry Street from Capel Street direction and had halted just opposite our position. It had come down noiselessly and we had not noticed it until it was right opposite to us. I knew it would be no use opening rifle or revolver fire on it, and we had no bombs. I immediately sent to the GPO for bombs and for a couple of men who knew how to use them. The bombs we used at that time were very crude, they were tin-cans of different sizes filled with some kind of ready-made shrapnel, and a long piece of fuse protruded from the top. A match had to be lit and the fuse ignited in this way. None of our men had any experience with bombs, and I was very anxious that men with some experience would come along to use them, as I knew there had been some accidents already in the GPO when the men attempted to use bombs. Two men arrived quickly. The occupants of the armoured car appeared to be unaware of our presence, and I gave orders for absolute silence to be maintained. Before the two men who arrived had sufficient time to ignite their bombs, the armoured car moved back towards Capel Street to its original position. I reported this episode to GHQ.

About this time I was told that Commandant Edward Daly,[44] who was in command of the Four Courts area, was endeavouring to link up with us, and I was ordered to keep a sharp look out for his men and to render them, if they came, all the assistance I could. While watching for his party, we observed that the enemy had arrived at the junction of Parnell Street and Moore Street. An officer appeared at first and must have been under the impression that we were not occupying the buildings dominating Moore Street. He appeared to be supervising some task which he had allotted to his men, probably the erection of a barricade. I had this position covered immediately by as many riflemen as we could get into position, and I withheld fire for some time in the hope of getting a large target. Eventually as it appeared as if the enemy were about to get under cover, I gave the order to fire and some casualties were inflicted, including the officer. We allowed his men to carry the officer away. After that the enemy withdrew from that position and we saw no more of them that day.

I made frequent visits to GHQ to report progress generally. I saw Pearse, Connolly, Tom Clarke, Joseph Plunkett,[45] The O'Rahilly[46] and Seán McDermott.[47]

As night approached, it was apparent that the fires which had been caused by the enemy were increasing in volume, and were getting nearer to us. I went up on the roof of the GPO in the darkness to get an idea of the position, and found that we were practically surrounded by fires.

Some time during the night of Thursday I got an order from GHQ to withdraw all my men to the GPO, as an attack on the main position appeared to be imminent. Our men were allowed a short rest and were then allocated to different posts in the GPO buildings facing O'Connell Street.

From that on I was in the position of being an officer attached to GHQ Staff, without any particular task to do except what would result from the trend of events.

At this time O'Connell Street appeared to be a blazing inferno. The fires were terrific. The roaring of the flames, the noise of breaking glass and of the collapsing walls was terrific. The flames from the Imperial Hotel and from Hoyte's drug and oil stores at the corner of Sackville Place were so fierce that they almost touched the walls of the GPO, and we could feel the heat of them.

That brings us to Friday.

Enemy fire, including sniping, was becoming more intense, and with a few of my own men I went up on to the roof of the GPO to reinforce our snipers who were there. We spent several hours of the early morning exchanging shots with the enemy snipers.

Later in the morning all the members of the Cumann na mBan were ordered to leave the building, which they did very regretfully. They had a splendid field hospital in a room in the GPO, and had prepared food for the garrison from the beginning of the occupation of the GPO.

During the afternoon of Friday, incendiary bombs set the roof of the GPO on fire. The flames spread rapidly over the roof, and the building was soon burning around us.

James Connolly at this time was suffering from severe wounds in his leg and was on a stretcher, from which he commanded the garrison. This was in the main hall of the GPO facing O'Connell Street. Hoses were used to try to extinguish the flames, but the hoses were useless.

The whole garrison was then ordered to assemble in the main hall, and were told that an evacuation was about to take place. That would probably be coming on towards six o'clock in the evening. It was believed at the time that the British would attack on foot from the direction of Lower Abbey Street, as they were known to be in force there and in Marlboro' Street. When the garrison assembled in the main hall they got ready to cope with such an attack, and although everything seemed pretty hopeless at the time, the spirit of the men was magnificent and the whole garrison sang The Soldiers' Song in a spontaneous outburst. There was a suggestion of making a burst through to Parnell Street and seizing Williams & Woods factory.

The position from the fires was very serious by this time, and the evacuation had to proceed as quickly as possible. The building was almost empty when Seán McDermott, who was near me at the time, exclaimed that the men in the Metropole Hotel had been forgotten and were in danger of being left behind. He asked for a volunteer to see that the men in the Metropole were withdrawn and that they followed the main body, which had gone across Henry Street and into Henry Place and Moore Street. I undertook this task, as I was unattached, and McDermott impressed upon me that I was to make sure that no member of the garrison of the Metropole Hotel was left behind.

I got in touch with Oscar Traynor, who was in charge of the Metropole Hotel garrison, and he succeeded in bringing all his men in safety to the GPO under cover of a barricade in Prince's Street. That barricade was directly in front of where the Capitol Theatre and the Prince's Bar is now, and communicated with a large gate leading into the GPO.

Before the general evacuation of the GPO began, the wounded were moved first to the Coliseum Theatre and later were brought to Jervis Street Hospital.

After I had got in touch with Oscar Traynor I was ordered by Diarmuid Lynch[48] to assist in bringing all the explosives to the basement of the GPO. Diarmuid Lynch was an officer attached to GHQ. About half a dozen of us took part in this job, and we brought grenades and other explosives down some long passage into the cellars of the GPO. Owing to the amount of water that had been poured on to the roof, we were working in the wet and were drenched through.

When all the explosives had been placed in the cellars we retired to the door of the GPO in Henry Street, facing Henry Place. The shooting down Henry Street at this time was very intense, and for a long time it was impossible to cross the road. In our little party, which numbered about a dozen, were P. H. Pearse and Willie Pearse. I believe that P. H. Pearse had already been across the street into Henry Place, but had returned to make sure that everything was in order. One of the Plunketts, I believe it was George Plunkett,[49] was also in our party.

P. H. Pearse, while we were waiting near the door, said that he would take a final look round the GPO to make absolutely certain that nobody had been left behind. He was away for a long time, and we were getting nervous lest he had been hit by some of the bullets which were coming in through the windows at the time. While we were waiting we heard steps coming down one of the passages, and a man whom I knew to be Séamus Kavanagh, and who was lame, opened the door, put his head out and asked us was anything wrong. He explained that owing to his lameness he had been given some duties of a clerical nature for some of the GHQ officers, that he had been overcome with fatigue, got into a corner somewhere and fell asleep, and was unaware of the evacuation. Pearse eventually came back and stated that nobody appeared to be in the building. During lulls in the enemy firing we dashed across Henry Street in ones and twos. The bullets appeared to be striking the ground at our feet as we rushed across.

I am certain that our party was the very last to leave the GPO.

When we got across the street, there was a cry that we were being attacked, and we threw down a rough barricade of whatever was at hand, to fire from in case the British came down the lane after us. George Plunkett was along with me at this hastily erected barricade. However, there was no attack. It was beginning to get dark at this time.

There was great confusion in Henry Place. A couple of men were killed by stray shots from the enemy, and one man, Henry Coyle, a member of my own Company, was killed when trying to burst open a door with his rifle, which was loaded. After some time I noticed that Seán McLoughlin appeared to be taking command. I tried my best to restore order amongst the men in the rear of the column, and McLoughlin told me that he had been given command and was placing me in charge of the rearguard. I established my party in a bottling stores at the corner of the lane which runs parallel to O'Connell Street and Moore Street as far as the Rotunda Hospital.

The men at this time were suffering very much from cold and hunger, and we had no food of any description with us. For the first time during the week I noticed that it was a bit hard to control the men, and I decided that the best thing to do would be to get them some hot drinks and food. I saw to my dismay that the building we were in had a stone floor and not even a water tap in it. I noticed that at the junction of Henry Place and Moore Street some of our men were going to and fro with kettles of hot water, so I decided that I would go there and see what I could get. Sniping was going on around us and we had to be pretty careful. I placed Charles Rossiter in charge of the rearguard during my absence and told him and the men what I was going to do and that I would be back soon with food and hot drinks. I then went off to the house at the corner of Moore Street, and I must have collapsed here, because I remember nothing else until I woke up lying on the floor in the darkness. I found, when daylight came, that I was in a house at the Southern corner of the junction of Henry Place and Moore Street.

I went out into Henry Place and found that the rearguard party had been withdrawn from the stores I had occupied the previous night. In a short time I saw Seán McDermott, who told me that our men during the night had bored through the houses in Moore Street in a Northerly direction towards Parnell Street. At the junction of these two streets the British had erected a barricade which was manned. He said that, in order to draw the attention of the British off the men who were boring through, he wanted a 'mock barricade' erected where we were, at the junction of Moore Street and Henry Place. I took charge of this operation, and, with the aid of ropes, we ran out a cart into the middle of Moore Street. We also threw out boxes and everything else we could find. We managed to fill a couple of sacks with clay and placed them in position at the corner. Immediately the cart appeared the British opened fire, which was very intense. Amongst the men who fired from the barricade were the late Harry Boland and Tom McGrath recently deceased.[50] Shots were exchanged for a period, the duration of which I cannot now estimate. At one period during the firing, some kind of a missile fell beside our barricade. I was told afterwards that this was an incendiary bomb which did not explode.

About this time we made efforts to get some food, but there appeared to be no food ready for consumption. A few tins of sardines and a small amount of chocolate were got, but this was not sufficient for the men. There were sacks of flour in one of the shops we occupied, but we had no means of preparing anything to eat with the flour.

About midday Seán McDermott told us that a truce had been arranged and that officers on both sides were discussing the details. He gave us strict instructions to remain very quiet, not to expose ourselves to fire, and to be careful not to fire any shots ourselves during the duration of the truce, as he was quite sure that there were many among the enemy who would avail of any excuse to open fire on us again.

Previous to this the British had been firing down Moore Street indiscriminately when anybody appeared on the street. Many civilians who lived in the small streets and lanes off Moore Street were killed at this time.

Later in the afternoon Seán McDermott told us that agreement had been reached and that we were surrendering as prisoners of war. I believe he said that we were surrendering unconditionally, but this has been disputed. Accordingly, we filed out into Moore Street with our arms and ammunition, formed up under our officers, and marched off with our rifles at the slope, through Moore Street, Henry Place into Henry Street and Upper O'Connell Street, as far as the portion extending from the Gresham Hotel to Parnell Street corner. We were all lined up on the East side of O'Connell Street. I happened to be beside Joseph Plunkett; beside him were Tom Clarke and Seán McDermott. We were all lined up facing the opposite, i.e. the West, side of O'Connell Street, and were ordered to throw down our arms and ammunition in a heap on the road. I noticed at this time that there was a gaping hole in the wall of the CYMS, which was almost opposite. It appears that it was struck by a shell.

Our names were taken by British officers, many of whom were very truculent. There was one of them who behaved like a soldier and a gentleman. Joseph Plunkett was singled out by one British officer for particular insult. Plunkett was ordered to step forward from the ranks, and he was ignominiously searched. He had his Will in his pocket, and the British officer passed some very rude remarks about Plunkett's courage, asking him was he making his Will because he was afraid he would die. I remarked at the time that Joseph Plunkett paid not the slightest heed to what this British officer said to him. He had been talking to us in the ranks before the incident about the Rising generally, its effect, and about some steps he had taken in regard to publicity in foreign lands. When he had been maltreated by this officer, he stepped back into the ranks and resumed his conversation exactly where he had left off.

One of the Volunteers, named Henry Ridgeway, was wearing a Red Cross armlet on his uniform, and he was picked out of the ranks by a British officer who asked him what he was wearing on his arm. Ridgeway told the officer, who said, 'I don't recognise your d—— Red Cross', and tore off the armlet with a bayonet.

Our arms and ammunition were thrown down in a heap in the middle of the road. Some men broke their weapons before they threw them down. We were also ordered to throw down any ammunition we had and to empty our pockets of everything that was in them. Our names and addresses were then taken.

About this time it was getting dark, and I noticed on the far side of the street a small number of men in a strange uniform which appeared to be of a very light green colour. Tom Clarke, who was near me, said that he wondered if these were the men of Casement's Brigade. We had heard rumours during the week that the Germans had landed some troops, and Clarke's remarks left me under the impression that he believed the Germans had succeeded in landing some troops which included the men of Casement's Brigade. At a later period I formed the impression that these men were members of the Local Reserve of old time soldiers whom the British had got together in Dublin, popularly known as the 'Gorgeous Wrecks'. This name was taken from the wording on their epaulettes — Georgius Rex.[51]

There were no citizens on the street at this time, but I noticed that there were some people in civilian dress in the Gresham Hotel who were at the windows looking on at what was taking place.

I should have mentioned that we left behind in Moore Street a few wounded men who were later picked up by the British Medical Unit. Most of these were only slightly wounded. There was one man, however, seriously wounded, Joe Kenny of 'B' Company, 2nd Battalion, who never properly recovered. He was severely wounded in the leg.

We were marched over to the green plot inside the railings of the Rotunda Hospital, in front of the main entrance. We were not long there until we were joined by the garrison of the Four Courts area, amongst whom was Ned Daly, the Commandant of the area, and Fionán Lynch.[52] The area of the green plot was extremely small, and we were ordered on no account to stir off the grass but to keep lying down there. Accordingly, we were actually on top of one another. The night spent there can be described without any exaggeration as a night of horror.

Tom Clarke was maltreated shortly after we arrived at the plot. He was taken away somewhere for a while and many of the men around me told me that his boots were taken off, although I did not actually see that happening. At one period I noticed Michael Collins[53] protesting vigorously to the British officers at the maltreatment of Tom Clarke. The conduct of many of the British officers during the night can only be described as savage. In particular, Captain Lea-Wilson, who was later shot during the Black and Tan period in Wexford, was brutal. Some of the Dublin Metropolitan Police also uttered sundry threats during the night, but one or two of them were inclined to be rather decent. There were three or four women amongst the prisoners, and they also had to spend the night along with the rest of us on the green plot. I forget the names of the women who were there. James Connolly's secretary, who died a few years ago, was one of the three or four women who were there. She was from Belfast and her family name was, I think, Carney.[54] We received no water and no food during the whole night. Several times, British officers and other ranks came around jibing at us about what was going to happen to us, and asking us if we would like food, or if we would like smokes, etc.

All during the night there was intermittent firing from the tower of the Rotunda Hospital, which was occupied by British troops. During the night we could also hear the shrieks of the patients inside, who appeared to have gone out of their minds.

Early in the morning, some time after daybreak, we were ordered to stand up and to get ready to march off. At this time Seán McDermott's stick, without which he could not walk, was taken from him and he was obliged to lean on the shoulder of whoever was next to him in the ranks. A DMP officer, to whom McDermott said that he was unable to walk without his stick, asked him what he was doing in an insurrection, and Seán replied that there was work for everybody to do in the movement.

We marched down O'Connell Street, which was still burning on both sides. A flag was still flying from one corner of the GPO. As far as

I can remember it was a tri-colour, flying at the Prince's Street corner, but I am not quite certain. It appeared to be sticking out horizontally from the corner of the building. When we reached O'Connell Bridge I noticed that there was a big gaping hole in the centre of the bridge. This appeared to be the result of the explosion of gas-pipes. We continued down Westmoreland Street, College Green and Dame Street. In Dame Street I noticed that there were a few civilians about, and these people cursed us as we went by. We continued up Cork Hill, Christchurch Place, Thomas Street and James's Street.

When passing the Catholic Church in James's Street there was a priest inside the railings, as well as a great number of people who apparently had been attending Mass. At this point I noticed some priests of the Capuchin Order going by in some sort of a British Army vehicle. They were going in the direction of Inchicore. I think Father Aloysius was one of them. As there was firing going on in this vicinity, we made a detour down Steevens' Lane, and turned into John's Road.

When we came near the Islandbridge end of John's Road, I noticed a number of British soldiers in the grounds of the Royal Hospital, Kilmainham. These soldiers shouted to us that our friends the Germans had been heavily defeated in several battles, and that many of their ships had been sunk.

We continued via Kilmainham to Richmond Barracks. There were a few civilians knocking around in the vicinity of the barracks. During the whole march we had not been allowed any food or water. There was a very heavy escort of military, almost two to every prisoner. The soldiers were mainly of the Royal Irish Rifles. A great many of them were from Belfast and were very unfriendly. Amongst them, however, were some men from other Counties in Ireland who were inclined to be sympathetic and who handed their water bottles around. The soldiers who did this were abused by the other soldiers.

When we got into the barrack square we were halted and searched several times. Some of the searches were official and some of them were carried out by the soldiers themselves for the purpose of getting money, tobacco and other personal belongings from the prisoners.

After standing in the square for a long period, the length of which I cannot now estimate, we were brought into a room which they called 'the gymnasium'. Before we entered this room we had to pass through a kind of turnstile, where every man was scrutinised by DMP [Dublin Metropolitan Police] and military officers, who picked out leaders and other men against whom they were about to bring charges. These men were put in a corner of the room separate to the main body. Amongst those picked out were Tom Clarke, Joe Plunkett, Seán McDermott, Seán McGarry,[55] Fionán Lynch and my brother, Leo Henderson.

We were kept lying on the floor for a long time and eventually water was brought in to us in buckets, and we got some hard biscuits to eat. We were then locked in the room.

Pearse was not with our party, as he had been taken away at the time of the surrender. James Connolly had been removed on a stretcher from Moore Street. The stretcher was carried by Volunteers, one of whom was Séamus Devoy.

From time to time a British officer or a DMP man would come into the room where we were and have a look at us. Some of the DMP men picked out a few of our men and put them amongst the special group. These people who came to look at us were all very unfriendly. Later in the evening, however, the door was opened by a private soldier who told us he was from Co. Clare. He wanted to know what he could do for us. He was very friendly, and brought in buckets of drinking water.

Rumours began to get around then that we were going to be sent to the Curragh, or out to France to dig trenches.

At one period somebody suggested that we ourselves should go through our pockets and see if we had any documents. I discovered then that I had a copy of a dispatch I had sent to James Connolly from Fairview, and also the dispatch that James Connolly had sent to me, ordering us to withdraw from Fairview. These papers had escaped the several searchers. I regretted that I had to destroy these documents, which was a difficult thing to do because in the one grate in the room there was just the smouldering remains of a fire which barely sufficed to burn the papers, and all matches had been taken from us.

As it was getting dusk in the evening we were all — except the special group which had been picked out by the British military and police — ordered out to the barrack square, and were told that we were about to be moved off somewhere. They served us with tins of bullybeef and a few hard biscuits, and told us that we were to be careful with this food as it was all we would get for some time. While we were in the barrack square, more Republican prisoners were marched in, including the garrison from Jacobs and the College of Surgeons.

It was getting dark when we marched off. We marched out of the barracks and turned towards Kingsbridge. To the best of my recollection the route we followed to Kingsbridge was via James's Street and Steevens' Lane. We crossed the Liffey either at Kingsbridge or at the next bridge nearer the city and marched along the North side Quays until we got to Grattan Bridge. By this time it was completely dark and there were no street lamps lighting. All the houses and shops were in darkness and the streets were deserted. We re-crossed the Liffey at Grattan Bridge and continued as far as Butt Bridge, where we crossed again and proceeded along the North Wall as far as the L&NWR station, whence we proceeded by the underground passage to a steamer which was waiting for us.

All along the route, in addition to our escort, which consisted of a double line of troops on both sides of the column, there were detachments of soldiers, even in the underground passage. During the march from the barracks to the boat, a few of the British soldiers passed round their water bottles to us. During our march there were occasional sounds of rifle and machine gun fire. This firing did not appear to be very close to us.

When we got to the steamer we had a very good view of the burning city. We were immediately put down into the cattle lairs. British soldiers were posted all round the ship and challenged us any time we made a move. There was talk of submarines being in the Bay. I fell asleep soon after the boat left the Quay, and I do not remember anything more until we arrived at Holyhead.

We disembarked at Holyhead and went immediately into a train which was waiting for us. This would be about midnight or very early in the morning of 1st May.

Apparently we had been divided into two parties, for, while one lot went to Knutsford jail, the party I was with arrived eventually at Stafford station at about seven o'clock in the morning. We were lined up in the square outside Stafford station, and a crowd of civilians began to assemble and pass insulting remarks. A couple of them attacked some of our men. A British NCO, Staff Sergeant Shaw, at this point seized hold of one of the attackers, pushing him away and said, 'These men at any rate had the courage to fight.'

We were marched then towards the jail. On the way there we were heartened by seeing some of the posters of the morning papers, one of which referred to the 'Seven Days War'. The fact that they referred to our fight as a 'War' helped to cheer us somewhat. We also saw the announcement, 'Fall of Kut',[56] on a poster.

We were marched into Stafford jail. This jail was composed mainly of two separate buildings, one known as 'The Crescent' and the other as 'The New Prison'. We were marched into the portion known as the Crescent. Before the war it had been a women's jail, but had been turned into a military detention prison. Military prisoners had been cleared out to make room for us. After being medically examined and our names taken, we were shown our cells, warned not to talk or attempt to communicate in any way with one another, and locked in.

Amongst the prisoners in Stafford jail with us were Michael Collins, Murt O'Connell, Denis Daly from Cahirciveen, Seán Flood, Brian O'Higgins, Seán MacEntee[57] who was later taken away from the jail and brought back to Ireland for court martial, and at a later period Darrell Figgis[58] and Herbert Moore Pim.[59]

For one month we were locked in our cells almost for the whole time, with the exception of about an hour's exercise every day. The British military here, with one or two exceptions, were very decent men. The Staff Sergeant, to whom I referred earlier, an old soldier who had volunteered for the War while he was in America, told me at one period that he had been supplied with batons before we arrived, and told to expect the worst possible type of ruffians. He told me that he had replied that he had soldiered for a good many years in Ireland and had found Irishmen generally not of that type, and that he would give them a chance before he would use the batons.

The first Sunday after our arrival we were not allowed to go to Mass, but on the second Sunday we attended Mass, which was celebrated in the prison church. Military guards were all over the church during Mass, and the priest, Father Moore, who afterwards became a very kind friend to us, referred during his sermon to our 'crime', etc. Later during the week Father Moore came amongst us, and, having had some conversation with us, changed his opinion of us and became a very warm friend of ours. Although his name was Moore he was not of Irish descent; he told us that he belonged to an English family of Moores. There was also a Canon Keating whom we saw on a few occasions, but, although a very priestly man, he had not the slightest sympathy with us and did not understand anything about us.

After one month's solitary confinement, during which period some of us got jobs to do which occupied us a good deal during the day, such as cutting bread, serving meals, etc., we were allowed free association with one another, and our cells were unlocked night and day.

There were four landings in this portion of the jail, and our organisation at the time was that we had two leaders on each landing.

During this second month we were allowed to receive parcels from home, to see visitors, and to buy extra food if we had the money.

The first news we had of the executions was about a fortnight after our arrival, when we were told verbally by Staff Sergeant Shaw that some of our leaders had been shot. Other than that we did not get any news for the first three or four weeks.

When we were allowed to associate with one another we began to see our fellow-prisoners in the other portion of the jail known as the New Prison. They consisted mainly of men from Galway and other parts of the country, a few from Dublin city and Dublin County.

About the beginning of July we learned that we would be moved to a camp at Frongoch in North Wales.[60] We went there by train in batches of fifty or so. Before we were moved, those of us who were in uniform were told that we would have to leave our uniforms behind, and we were served out with suits of clothes of very poor material and very bad fit, known as 'Henry Martins'. Before being sent to Frongoch we were all moved over to the other portion of the jail.

Nothing eventful happened during our journey to Frongoch. The particular party that I was in arrived at about six or seven o'clock in the evening at the portion of the camp known as the North Camp. This portion of the camp was composed of wooden huts. The South Camp, which was quite close to the North Camp, was a converted disused distillery. Both portions of the camp had been used previous to our arrival as an internment camp for German prisoners.

On arriving at the camp we were addressed by the British Adjutant, who read out the rules and regulations to us. We also had a short address from Sergeant Major Newsome, who was nicknamed 'Jack Knives' by our men. Although his address to us was full of threats for breaches of camp regulations, our experience of 'Jack Knives' afterwards showed us that he was a very kindly although very rough-mannered man.

Inside the camp itself the running of things was left to ourselves, subject, of course, to inspections by the British Commandant. When I arrived, M. W. O'Reilly was our Camp Commandant in the North Camp. We were allotted to huts which held about twenty-five men each. Each hut immediately elected a hut leader, who was responsible to the British authorities under their regulations, and also to our own Commandant under our own regulations. The huts were inspected every morning by the British Commandant, accompanied by our own Commandant. Fire precautions included the forming of a volunteer fire brigade from amongst us. We also organised concerts, etc. Under Prisoner of War rules we were entitled to select certain of our men for working parties in connection with the camp work, and these men received prisoner of war pay from the British.

While these working parties were carrying out their tasks around the camp, some breaches of the regulations occurred and the men involved in them, along with our own Camp Commandant, were charged before the British Commandant and penalised by being put in the guard-room. Paddy Daly, later Major General Daly, was one of those penalised. He immediately went on hunger-strike, which secured the release of all the men who had been put into the guard-room, but resulted in the removal of M. W. O'Reilly to Reading jail along with some other men from both the North Camp and the South Camp.

The British military chaplain attached to the camp was Father Stafford, a Dublin man.

Batches of men were released from time to time, until about the end of July when we were told there would be no more releases, and we were then all moved down to the South Camp. There were about enough men left to fill either of the camps.

Shortly after we went down to the South Camp, the British Adjutant read out a communication concerning us which he had received from his authorities. This communication stated that we were going to be treated as prisoners of war but that we were not prisoners of war, that we belonged, as prisoners, to the Home Office, and that they were handing us over to the War Office for the purpose of our internment, but that the Home Office might take us back again. This was a very long communication, and when the Adjutant had finished reading it the whole camp burst into the song, 'We're here because we're here'.

I should have mentioned that before the releases started we were all brought by train in batches from Frongoch to London to appear before a Tribunal presided over by Judge Sankey.[61] At this Tribunal we were asked questions about the part we had taken in the Rising. Most of the questions seemed to be directed to getting us to make a confession of being misled by our leaders and being sorry for what we had done. The journey from Frongoch to London and back occupied three days. In London we were kept at Wandsworth Prison and the Tribunal sat in one of the offices of the prison. Some of the other parties of our men when brought to London were kept at Wormwood Scrubs Prison, where the Tribunal also sat.

The British Commandant was a very tactless man, who was fond of taking up our leaders on small points, and this led to several encounters with him. The first encounter of any magnitude was one when the British authorities were apparently about to pick out any of our men who had been resident in England previous to the Rising, and who, under British law, were liable for military service. The men whose names were called out refused to answer and the British authorities made an attempt to segregate us. They picked out some of us whose names they thought they knew, but they were wrong in a great many cases.

We had gone back to the North Camp at this time, and those of us who were taken out from the main body were transferred to the South Camp. The men thus transferred would possibly be about a quarter of the whole number in the camp. I was amongst this number, and when we got down to the South Camp we decided to go on hunger-strike. We had brought down some food with us and it was agreed that we would finish up whatever food we had, and when it had been consumed we would commence the hunger-strike. This strike lasted for three days, during which time the British Commandant got frightened and did not come to inspect us in the mornings as was his habit. 'Jack Knives', who had shown his sympathy with us on a few occasions, cooked our food and implored us to take it, but, of course, we refused it. On the third day word was conveyed to us that we were being brought back to our comrades in the North Camp, and the hunger-strike was, accordingly, called off.

Shortly afterwards the British made a more determined attempt to remove our men who were liable for conscription, and they sent in a large body of troops who were distributed around the camp with fixed bayonets. The men were then ordered to their respective huts, and British officers went to each hut in turn calling out the names of the men. This had occurred so suddenly that there was not time to make any plan, but word had been got around to some of the huts to refuse to answer the names. It worked out that some huts did answer and others did not. In the long run, although it appeared to be dividing our forces at first, this proved to be of great benefit to us. The men who did not answer to their names were brought down under armed guard to the South Camp. These men were told that all their privileges would be removed, that they would not be allowed to write letters, receive parcels or anything else of that nature. When any of these men reported sick, the doctor was not allowed to give any treatment to them unless they gave their names. The doctor came round every morning, and as no names were given to him he was not allowed to carry out his duties. This appears to have driven the doctor out of his mind, and he was found drowned in the river shortly afterwards. He was a native of the district and not a military doctor.

As the prisoners' hospital was situated in the South Camp, and according to the British organisation the food, etc., for it was supplied from the North Camp rations, we were able to establish communications. A number of men who were genuinely sick were in hospital, and a ration party of our men came down three times every day from the North Camp surreptitiously carrying letters, tobacco, and all the things that the men who were penalised had been getting previously.

During all this time, both in the North and South Camps, the nucleus of the future IRA was being formed, mainly through the activities of the leading men of the IRB who were interned with us.

About three days before Christmas, the order came for our release, and we were sent home, the countrymen first and the city men later. With the exception of a few men who were too ill to travel, the Camp was cleared on the day before Christmas Eve, 1916.

Notes to Introduction

1   For such recent work see Joost Augusteijn, *From Public Defiance to Guerrilla Warfare: The Experience of Ordinary Volunteers in the Irish War of Independence, 1916–1921* (Dublin, 1996); Peter Hart, 'The Irish Republican Army and its Enemies: Violence and Community in Cork, 1917–1923' (Ph.D. thesis, Trinity College, Dublin, 1992); David Fitzpatrick, *Politics and Irish Life, 1913–1921: Provincial Experience of War and Revolution* (Dublin, 1977).

2   Writing to the editor on 27 Oct. 1996, Henderson's son stated: 'May I say that you can take each point at face value as my father was not only a very meticulous man, but also very truthful, of good memory, deeply involved and not a brag.'

3   O'Malley Notebooks, P17b/99 (University College, Dublin, Archives).

4   Ibid.

5   Oscar Traynor (1886–1963): born in Dublin; goalkeeper for Belfast Celtic; printer; OC Dublin Brigade IRA, 1920–22; anti-Treaty; interned in Gormanstown Camp; released, 1924; elected to Dáil, 1925; Minister for Posts and Telegraphs in Fianna Fáil government 1936; Minister for Defence, 1939; Minister for Justice at the time of IRA's Northern offensive, 1957; director of *Irish Press*. See Traynor Memoirs (written at request of President de Valera): de Valera Papers, 1527/2 (University College, Dublin, Archives); O'Malley Notebooks, P17b/96, 98; *Irish Press*, 16 Dec. 1963.

6   Harry (Henry) Colley (1891–1972): rate-collector; adjutant to Dublin Brigade, 1920–30; Fianna Fáil TD for North-East Dublin, 1944–57; father of George Colley (Tánaiste, 1977–81). See O'Malley Notebooks, P17b/97; NLI, MS 10915.

7   NLI, MS 10915.

8   Michael Hopkinson, *Green against Green: The Irish Civil War* (Dublin, 1988).

9   All biographical details relating to Frank Henderson appearing in this Introduction, and which are not substantiated by individual footnote references, are taken either from Henderson's own writings or from communications sent to the editor by the Henderson family in 1989 and 1996. Their letter of 19 Mar. 1996 also contains Josephine Henderson's account of her experiences in the Easter Rising.

10   Leo Henderson in O'Malley Notebooks, P17b/105.

11   Traynor Memoirs: de Valera Papers, 1527/2.

12   C. S. Andrews, *Dublin Made Me* (Dublin & Cork, 1979).

13   Mulcahy Memoirs: Mulcahy Papers, P7b/184 (University College, Dublin, Archives); Frank Henderson in O'Malley Notebooks, P17b/99; Traynor Memoirs: de Valera Papers, 1527/2; Frank Henderson, 'Irish Leaders of Our Time, 5: Richard McKee', *An Cosantóir*, v (1945), 301–11.

14   O'Malley Notebooks, P17b/99.

15   Ibid.; Hopkinson, *Green against Green*, pp. 145–6.

16 O'Malley Notebooks, P17b/99.
17 Frank Henderson, Senate election address, 7 Mar. 1938, pamphlet in Henderson Family Papers. Henderson was nominated on the Industry and Commerce panel.

Notes to Narrative

1   Order of the Cistercians of the Strict Observance.
2   Thomas O'Neill Russell (1828–1908): Gaelic revivalist, novelist; spent 30 years in USA; returned to Ireland, 1895.
3   William Rooney (1872/3–1901): poet, journalist, language revivalist.
4   Arthur Griffith (1871–1922): printer, writer, journalist; editor of the *United Irishman*, 1899; founded Sinn Féin organisation, 1906; interned after Easter Rising; Vice-President of Sinn Féin, 1917; Acting President of Dáil, 1919–20; headed Irish delegation at Anglo-Irish Treaty conference, 1921; President of Dáil, Jan. 1922.
5   David Patrick Moran (1869–1936): journalist, polemicist; founder and editor of *The Leader*.
6   The Duke and Duchess of York, though not the Queen herself, visited Dublin in August 1897, in celebration of Victoria's Diamond Jubilee. The Queen's fourth and final visit to Ireland occurred in April 1900.
7   Major John MacBride (1865–1916): organiser of Irish Brigade in Boer War; settled in Paris; married Maud Gonne; former representative for Connacht on Supreme Council of IRB, though not involved in planning Easter Rising; executed after the rising.
8   Seán O'Casey (1884–1964): socialist, playwright; member of Gaelic League, IRB, ITGWU, and on council of Irish Citizen Army.
9   Brian O'Higgins: interned in Frongoch after Easter Rising; elected TD for Clare, 1918.
10 James Connolly (1868–1916): Labour leader and Marxist revolutionary; born in Edinburgh; founded Irish Socialist Republican Party, 1896; in USA, 1902–9, where he co-founded International Workers of the World; organised ITGWU, 1910, and Irish Citizen Army, 1914; signatory to Proclamation of Irish Republic, 1916; executed after the rising.
11 William O'Brien (1881–1968): master builder; trade union leader; General Secretary, ITGWU, 1926–46.
12 John (Eoin) MacNeill (1867–1945): Gaelic scholar and Gaelic League organiser; Chief of Staff of Irish Volunteers at time of Easter Rising; MP and TD; Minister for Industries, 1919–21; Minister for Education, 1922–25; Free State member on Boundary Commission, 1925.

13   Patrick (Pádraic) Henry Pearse (1879–1916): trained as lawyer; schoolmaster; prominent member of Gaelic League; headmaster, St Enda's School; President of the Provisional Government of the Irish Republic and commandant-in-chief of its forces during Easter Rising; executed after the rising.

14   Thomas MacDonagh (1878–1916): Director of Training of Irish Volunteers; member of IRB Military Council; Assistant Lecturer, University College, Dublin; signatory to Proclamation of Irish Republic, 1916; executed after the rising.

15   Harry Boland (1887–1922): Member of Dublin 2nd Battalion; leading Sinn Féin organiser in Ireland and USA; TD; President of Supreme Council of IRB; shot in early stages of Civil War.

16   Eamonn Ceannt (1881–1916): clerk on staff of Dublin Corporation; founded Dublin Pipers' Club; member of IRB Military Council; signatory to Proclamation of Irish Republic, 1916; executed after the rising.

17   Robert Monteith (1880–1956): IRB man and Roger Casement's chief assistant in his Irish brigade enterprise.

18   Richard (Dick) McKee (1893–1920): printer; O/C Dublin Brigade, 1918–20; shot by British forces in Dublin Castle, Nov. 1920. See Frank Henderson, 'Irish Leaders of Our Time' 5: Richard McKee, *An Cosantoir*, v (1945), 301–11.

19   Peadar Clancy: leading member of Dublin Brigade; shot by British forces in Dublin Castle, Nov. 1920.

20   Eamon de Valera (1882–1975): born in New York; schoolmaster; member of Gaelic League and Volunteers; last surviving commandant of the Easter Rising; President of Sinn Féin, 1917–26; President of Dáil, 1919–22; opposed Treaty; established Fianna Fáil party, 1926; President of the Executive Council of Free State, 1932–37; Taoiseach, 1937–48, 1951–54, 1957–59; President of Irish Republic, 1959–73.

21   Jacob's Biscuit Factory was in Bishop Street on the western side of the city centre.

22   Patrick (Paddy) Moran: member of the Jacob's garrison, Easter Rising; interned after rising; convicted for alleged role in Bloody Sunday assasinations, Nov. 1920; hanged, 14 Mar. 1921.

23   Martin Savage: originally from Co. Sligo; shot dead during the attempted ambush of Lord French at Ashtown, Dec. 1919.

24   Saturday 22 Apr. 1916 was the date of these reports.

25   Roger Casement (1864–1916): member of the British colonial service, 1892–1912; joined Volunteers, 1913; attempted to establish an Irish brigade among prisoners of war in Germany; arrested on return to Ireland shortly before Easter Rising; tried for treason and executed in London.

26   Michael O'Hanrahan (1877–1916): journalist and Gaelic League activist; National Quartermaster of Volunteers; executed after the rising.

27 Paddy Daly: future leader of Collins's 'squad'; in charge of attack on Four Courts at beginning of Civil War, June 1922.

28 Eamon Price: Director of Organisation, GHQ IRA, at time of truce, July 1921; member of well-known Dublin republican family; founded Republican Congress, 1931.

29 See F. X. Martin (ed.), 'Eoin MacNeill on the 1916 Rising', *Irish Historical Studies*, xii (1961), pp. 226–71.

30 In his NLI Memoir Henderson wrote that the confusion over dates 'had a sickening effect upon the men'.

31 Thomas James Clarke (1857–1916): arrested for participation in dynamite campaign in England, 1883; released from jail, 1888; emigrated to USA, 1889; returned to Ireland, 1907; key figure within reorganised IRB, member of Supreme Council and of Military Council; signatory to Proclamation of Irish Republic, 1916; executed after the rising.

32 See also Henderson's NLI Memoir.

33 Seán Lester (1888–1959): journalist in Ireland until 1923; on staff of Department of External Affairs, 1923–39; Deputy Commissioner in Danzig, 1934–37; Deputy Secretary of League of Nations, 1937–40; Acting Secretary-General of League of Nations, 1940–45.

34 See also Henderson's NLI Memoir.

35 Both Henderson and Colley in their NLI Memoirs record how unpleasant the task was of removing the old woman and her daughter.

36 Seán Russell (1893–1940): interned after Easter Rising, 1916; Director of Munitions, GHQ IRA, 1920; anti-Treaty; active in IRA post-ceasefire; IRA Quartermaster-General, 1936; mainspring behind IRA bombing campaign in Britain, 1939; died *en route* to Ireland in German U-boat.

37 In his NLI Memoir Henderson describes this as 'a bad mistake'.

38 In his NLI Memoir Henderson wrote: 'The sight that met us when we were inside the PO was inspiring. Men were at the windows shooting while numbers were lying about wounded. Everything was business-like and there was an air of suppressed excitement.'

39 Henderson's NLI Memoir says eight men.

40 Eimar O'Duffy (1893–1935): dentist and writer; journalist in Paris.

41 Tom Ennis: commandant of 2nd Batallion, Dublin Brigade, 1920; wounded in attack on Custom House, 25 May 1921; served in Free State army.

42 Seán Kerr: purser on shipping line; agent for Michael Collins in Liverpool; arms-runner; arrested and imprisoned, 1920.

43 Seán Milroy (1877–1946): Sinn Féin journalist and TD; pro-Treaty.

44 Edward Daly (1891–1916): executed after the rising.

45 Joseph Plunkett (1887–1916): son of Count Plunkett; Director of Organisation,

Irish Volunteers, 1913; helped Casement with regard to plans for rising; member of IRB Supreme Council and Military Council; signatory to Proclamation of Irish Republic, 1916; executed after the rising.

46 Michael Joseph Rahilly (The O'Rahilly) (1875–1916): merchant's son from Kerry; journalist; member of Central Executive of Gaelic League; Director of Arms, Irish Volunteers, Nov. 1913; participated in Easter Rising although opposed to it; shot dead during the rising.

47 Seán McDermott (1884–1916): key member of reorganised IRB post-1910; member of IRB Military Council; signatory to Proclamation of Irish Republic, 1916; executed after the rising.

48 Diarmuid Lynch (1878–1950): participated in Easter Rising; President of Supreme Council, IRB; elected TD, 1918; emigrated to USA, where he became secretary of Friends of Irish Freedom.

49 George Plunkett (d. 1940): Irish Volunteer; interned, 1916; member of IRA GHQ, 1922–40.

50 In his NLI Memoir Henderson wrote that Boland 'showed amazing courage. He fired away by himself for a long time.'

51 The 'Georgius Rex' were the British army's Volunteer Defence Corps. They were returning from a route march in the countryside ignorant of events in the city. Five of them were killed and nine wounded in the confrontation.

52 Fionán Lynch (1889–1966): Kerry Volunteer; pro-Treaty TD, 1921–44; Minister for Education and for Fisheries, 1923–27; judge.

53 Michael Collins (1890–1922): emigrated to London from Co. Cork when fifteen; joined IRB and GAA; participated in GPO during Easter Rising; released from internment, Dec. 1916; key figure in reorganised IRB and Volunteers; Director of Organisation and of Intelligence in IRA during Anglo-Irish War; Minister for Finance in Dáil government, 1919–21; organised guerrilla warfare in Dublin, 1919–21; member of Irish delegation which signed Anglo-Irish Treaty, 1921; Chairman of Provisional Government and Commander-in-Chief of its army, July 1922; killed in ambush, 22 Aug. 1922.

54 Winifred Carney (1887–1943): trade unionist, socialist, feminist and republican; secretary of Textile Workers' Union in Belfast; personal secretary of James Connolly; interned after Easter Rising; Sinn Féin electoral candidate in Belfast, 1918; supported Republican side in Civil War; worked for ITGWU in Belfast and Dublin until 1928; active in radical wing of Northern Ireland Labour Party.

55 Seán McGarry: President of Supreme Council of IRB, Nov. 1917; General Secretary of Irish Volunteers, Nov. 1917; escaped from Lincoln jail with de Valera, Feb. 1919.

56 On 29 April 1916 the Turks captured Kut-el-Amara in Mesopotamia.

57 Seán MacEntee (1889–1980): originally from Belfast; involved in guerrilla action

on way to Dublin, 1916; TD, 1919–22; Minister for Finance in Fianna Fáil governments.

58   Darrell Figgis (1882–1925): journalist, author, Sinn Féin organiser and TD.

59   Herbert Moore Pim (1883–1934): from Belfast; novelist and poet of nationalist sympathies.

60   For Frongoch see Seán O'Mahony, *Frongoch: University of Revolution* (Dublin, 1987).

61   Judge (later Lord) Sankey was Chairman of the Detention Review Committee established in June 1916. Nearly 2,000 internees were brought to London to appear before the tribunal.

Bibliography

Andrews, C. S., *Dublin Made Me: An Autobiography* (Dublin & Cork, 1979)

Augusteijn, Joost, *From Public Defiance to Guerrilla Warfare: The Experience of Ordinary Volunteers in the Irish War of Independence, 1916–1921* (Dublin, 1996)

Brennan-Whitmore, W. J., *With the Irish in Frongoch* (Dublin, 1917)

Coogan, T. P., *Michael Collins* (London, 1990)

Dalton, Charles, *With the Dublin Brigade, 1917–1921* (London, 1929)

Dublin's Fighting Story, 1916–1921 (Tralee, 1949)

Fitzpatrick, David, *Politics and Irish Life, 1913–1921: Provincial Experience of War and Revolution* (Dublin, 1977)

Garvin, Tom, *Nationalist Revolutionaries in Ireland, 1859–1928* (Oxford, 1987)

Hart, Peter, 'The Irish Republican Army and its Enemies: Violence and Community in Cork, 1917–1923' (Ph.D. thesis, Trinity College, Dublin, 1992)

Hopkinson, Michael, *Green against Green: The Irish Civil War* (Dublin, 1988)

Mac Eoin, Uinseann (ed.), *Survivors* (Dublin, 1981; repr., Dublin, 1987)

Martin, F. X. (ed.), *The Irish Volunteers, 1913–1915: Recollections and Documents* (Dublin, 1963)

O'Doherty, Liam, 'Dublin – 1920', *Capuchin Annual* (1970), pp. 528–32

O'Mahony, Seán, *Frongoch: University of Revolution* (Dublin, 1987)

O'Malley, Ernie, *On Another Man's Wound* (London, 1936; repr., Dublin, 1979)

Townshend, Charles, *The British Campaign in Ireland, 1919–1921: The Development of Political and Military Policies* (Oxford, 1975)

Index

An Englishwoman in Belfast
Rosamond Stephen's Record of the Great War

Edited by *Oonagh Walsh*

Rosamond Stephen (1868–1951) was an Englishwoman who spent most of her life unsuccessfully trying to reconcile Protestants and Catholics in Ireland. The daughter of a theist judge, and niece of Sir Leslie Stephen, editor of the *Dictionary of National Biography*, she was received into the Church of Ireland in 1896 and worked as a lay missionary in working-class Belfast. Her attempts to meet, assist and talk politics with Belfast Catholics aroused suspicion in both communities, and her ecumenical quest ended in disillusionment.

This selection from her wartime letters to her sisters records her unique approach to philanthropy, her fervent support for the war effort, and her growing disgust with the British administration of Ireland. The editor's introduction reveals the frustration of a Unionist who viewed the Great War as a lost opportunity for reconciliation. Her letters apply an idiosyncratic moral perspective to Ireland's political history.

Oonagh Walsh teaches History at the University of Aberdeen.

1 85918 270 4   €11.50/£9.06 PB

A Policeman's Ireland

Recollections of Samuel Waters, R.I.C.

Edited by *Stephen Ball*

Samuel Waters followed his father and grandfather into the Irish Constabulary, rising from district inspector in 1866 to assistant inspector-general. His colourful and unembittered recollections encompass the Fenian Rising, The Land War and the 1916 insurrection, after which he retired to Skerries in Co. Dublin.

These memoirs illuminate the intelligence work of the R.I.C., as well as the social and sporting compensations of a policeman's life in all four provinces. Waters records unexpectedly friendly interactions between police and army in which he had to restrain a group of Fenian fans from beating up his military opponents.

The editor's introduction highlights the problems of policing Ireland during a century and a half of turmoil, and explains why a policeman's job could be a relatively happy one!

Stephen Ball is completing a doctorate on the policing of the Irish Land War at Goldsmiths College, London.

1 85918 189 9   €11.50/£9.06 PB

'My Darling Danny'

Letters from Mary O'Connell to Her Son Daniel, 1830–1832

Edited by *Erin Bishop*

On 9 May 1830, fourteen year-old Daniel O'Connell Jr., son of the Liberator, left his comfortable home in Dublin to attend the Jesuit college at Clongowes Wood in County Kildare. Thus began a three-year correspondence between Danny Jr. and his mother, Mary O'Connell. Bursting with love and affection, illness and death, politics and scandal, these letters allow a brief glimpse at the relationship between mother and son in nineteenth-century Ireland. In addition, this collection documents a portion of an important juncture in the political career of Danny's father Daniel O'Connell. Returned for Clare in the 1828 by-election, the 'Liberator' took his seat in 1830 as the first Catholic Member of Parliament and for the next several years focused his attention on the parliamentary business carried out in London. The collection of letters between mother and son is doubly valuable; it offers insights into both the ordinary social history of nineteenth-century Ireland as well as the extraordinary and exciting political history of parliamentary politics and of Daniel O'Connell.

Erin I. Bishop is an American scholar who recently completed a doctoral thesis on the O'Connell family for the National University of Ireland

ISBN 1 85918 173 2   €11.50/£9.06 PB

The Rebel in His Family

Selected Papers of William Smith O'Brien

Edited by *Richard Davis* and *Marianne Davis*

William Smith O'Brien was an improbable revolutionary, ill at ease as a leader of the 1848 rising at Ballingarry, Co. Tipperary, and then as a convict languishing in Van Diemen's Land until 1854. His aristocratic background and demeanour, his late conversion to Repeal in 1843, and his refusal to engage in active politics during his final years in Ireland, have made him a perplexing figure for biographers as well as his contemporaries. His politics also perplexed and outraged his father's family, the O'Brien's of Dromoland in Co. Clare. Even so, as his extensive family correspondence reveals, O'Brien was never abandoned by the majority of his kinsfolk. The unpublished letters exchanged amongst the O'Brien family between 1819 and 1864 reveal an unexpectedly warm if sententious personality, striving to preserve his family status and affections amidst controversy and disgrace. The publication of these letters is a fitting memorial to one of Ireland's most elusive rebels.

Richard Davis, emeritus Professor of History at the University of Tasmania, has published widely on 1848 and other Irish topics. In collaboration with *Marianne Davis* he is preparing a biography of Smith O'Brien.

ISBN 1 85918 181 3 €11.50/£9.06 PB

Pádraig Ó Fathaigh's War of Independence

Recollections of a Galway Gaelic Leaguer

Edited by *Timothy G. McMahon*

Pádraig Ó Fathaigh (1879–1976) was a lifelong Gaelic Leaguer in Galway. Already an Irish volunteer before 1916, Ó Fathaigh was arrested on Easter Tuesday. He spent the next year undergoing penal servitude, the first of four terms of imprisonment between 1916 and 1920. When at liberty, he acted as an Intelligence Officer in South Galway and Mid-Clare. His hand-written recollections illuminate life 'on the run' and in prison, and will interest all students of the Irish Revolution and the Gaelic Revival.

Timothy G. McMahon lectures at the University Of Wisconsin

ISBN: 1 85918 145 7 €11.50/£9.06 PB

The Misfit Soldier

Edward Casey's War Story, 1914-1918

Edited by *Joanna Bourke*

Edward Casey, an underfed, under-sized and semi-literate Irish Cockney from Canning Town, was no war hero. Even so, his account of four years of war service with the Royal Dublin Fusiliers is a remarkable chronicle, revealing his personal and sexual insecurities, his remarkable experience of Irish unrest during periods of training and leave and his excitement as a military tourist in France, Salonica and Malta.

The memoir was written in 1980, six decades after his departure for New Zealand, yet retains a strong Cockney flavour. The editor has selected the chapters with the greatest interest for Irish readers, placing Casey's story in the broader context of the Great War and its sometimes devastating psychological consequences.

Joanna Bourke teaches history at Birkbeck College, London. Her books include *Dismembering the Male: Men's Bodies, Britain and the Great War* (1996)

ISBN: 1 85918 188 0   €11.50/£9.06 PB

Memoirs of Joseph Prost, C.Ss.R:

A Redemptorist Missionary in Ireland 1851-1854

Editors: *Emmet Larkin* and *Herman Freudenberger*

The recollections of Joseph Prost, an Austrian priest who initiated the Redemptorist parish missionary campaign in Ireland in 1851, provide a fascinating chronicle of the 'devotional revolution' by one of its most earnest organisers. Tireless and uncompromising in his determination to save souls and reinvigorate the Roman Catholic faith, Prost often came into conflict with the parish clergy and his Redemptorist brethren. Though writing from memory two decades after his departure from Ireland, Prost supplies a detailed account of religious practices and social mores just after the Great Famine in Limerick, Derry, Wexford and many other Irish towns. The text has been translated from the German and fully annotated, with an introductory essay on Prost's career and the development of the parish mission movement. The publication of this memoir is a major contribution to Irish religious and cultural history.

Emmet Larkin teaches British and Irish history at the University of Chicago, and has written numerous studies of Irish Catholicism. *Herman Freudenberger* is Professor Emeritus of Economic History at Tulane University, New Orleans , and has published extensively on the Hapsburg monarchy in the eighteenth and nineteenth centuries.

ISBN 1 85918 160 0   €11.50/£9.06

To Order:

Cork University Press, Crawford Business Park, Crosses Green, Cork, Ireland

Telephone our customer orderline	+353 (0)21 4902 980
Fax this order form directly	+353 (0)21 4315 329
E-mail your order to	corkunip@ucc.ie
Order on-line:	www.corkuniversitypress.com

Please add 15% of the total cost of the order to cover p&p in Ireland and the UK; add 25% for airmail orders

QTY	TITLE	PRICE
	An Englishwoman in Belfast	
	A Policeman's Ireland	
	'My Darling Danny'	
	The Rebel in his Family	
	Pádraig Ó Fathaigh's War of Independence	
	The Misfit Soldier	
	Memoirs of Joseph Prost, C.Ss.R	

p&p _____

Total _____

☐ I enclose a cheque made payable to Cork University Press.

☐ Please charge my credit card: Visa or Mastercard.

☐☐☐☐☐ ☐☐☐☐☐ ☐☐☐☐ ☐☐☐☐

Expiry Date ☐☐ ☐☐

Signature _____

Name _____

Address _____

Tel/e-mail _____

Printed in the United Kingdom
by Lightning Source UK Ltd.
130134UK00001B/139-204/P